PR
M000314440

NO LESS THAN YES

No Less Than Yes is a journey of trial and trust. It is a recounting of holding God's hand with faith—even in the hard times--and experiencing him working in marvelous and myriad ways for his children. It is the story of Dave and Connie Patty and their children, who dared to do this, and have seen Josiah Venture reach hundreds of thousands of Christian youth in the Czech Republic. This book will challenge and inspire Christ's followers who will say, "yes" to God, however and wherever he leads.

—*Anita Deyneka,*
Global Forum for a World Without Orphans

"While living in post-communist Europe in the 1990's being continually confronted with insurmountable odds and life-threatening circumstances, Connie Patty and her family faithfully responded with, "No less than Yes" to God's calling on their lives. Their captivating story of trusting God in the midst of heartache and fear, as well as astounding answers to prayer, will inspire and strengthen your faith."

—*Timothy Downey,*
Moody Bible Institute, Chicago.

Connie Patty takes readers on a journey filled with timely personal encounters with the promises of God. Prompted by the encouragement of her high school teacher after her name was not mentioned over the loudspeaker at her school as a winner in her class elections as she had hoped who said to her: "There is much more waiting for you," Connie tells her compelling personal story in response to God's call to engage in His mission to the world. In so doing she speaks to everyone who has experienced disappointment early in life to encourage them to embrace the promises of God from His Word which opens new vistas for our tomorrows. This story portrays Connie's missionary journey to the most non-religious atheistic nation in our world today, alongside of her husband Dave, where she becomes a catalyst of a youth discipling movement that is transforming society in the Czech Republic and surrounding European nations.

—*Luis Bush,*
Transform World Connections

Connie Patty's memoir reads like a fast-paced adventure novel, with Connie and Jesus as the main protagonists. In this powerfully written, deeply personal narrative, Connie shows what the Lord Jesus Christ can do in and through a young woman whose heart is willing to say 'Yes' to His call, in the midst of trials, heartaches and soaring victories, and in every season of life.

It is my privilege to have known Connie, a humble and beautiful woman of God, for over twenty years, and to have followed the amazing story of her family's life. Her story will thrill and encourage all believers. This is a must-read for young people considering missions as well as for all of us who long to say 'Yes' to the Lord.

—*Elizabeth Musser,*
Career Missionary and Novelist

In *No Less Than Yes*, Connie Patty has captured, with amazing precision and candor, God's story of faithfulness. Through personal and professional challenges, where despair and discouragement could have dislocated Josiah Venture from it's core mission, God is found faithful to His promises.

No Less Than Yes is a must read for all who seek to know God, hear His call, and act on His promises. You will not be disappointed.

—*David Sveen,*
Trustee, Domanada Foundation

no less than yes

PERSONAL ENCOUNTERS WITH
THE PROMISES OF GOD

Connie Patty

To my Josiah Venture family,
serving across Central and Eastern Europe
and
Dave, Tyler, Caleb and Claire,
who lived this story with me.

Trust in the Lord with all your heart
and lean not on your own understanding;
In all your ways acknowledge him,
and he will make your paths straight.
Proverbs 3:5-6 (NIV)

Contents

CHAPTER ONE *Called to Go*

"**I**f you are not called to be a missionary in the States, then you'd better ask the Lord where you ARE called to go."

Those words rang in my ears on a warm summer evening in June 1983 as I stood in the rafters of a university arena listening to Keith Green speak to thousands.

Days away from college graduation, I'd finished my last final in time to make it to the concert. However, this wasn't a live concert. Instead it was a video of his last performance before the tragic airplane crash that took his life, along with eleven others, including two of his own children.

His wife and ministry team were touring the United States the year after his death, speaking to young people on college campuses about Keith's challenge and legacy to live wholeheartedly for Jesus.

"*No Compromise* is what the whole Gospel of Jesus is all about. Deny yourself, take up your cross and follow him." — Keith Green, *No Compromise* album, 1978.

His challenge to forsake all and follow Jesus, particularly to the mission field, was utterly compelling to me that night. When he gave the invitation to stand in obedience to go wherever God asked me to go, I found myself rising to say yes to God and his plans for me.

Despite the fact that I'd never once considered going into the mission field.

Growing up in a small, rural Oregon town in the early 1960s, my exposure to missions consisted of infrequent visits by missionaries to the church I grew up in. Missionaries from Africa, Alaska and Idaho made their way to our little country church, but were far removed from the idyllic childhood I was in the middle of with my family.

Our world revolved around happy days in a small farming community, afternoons riding bikes with my brother and summers spent playing with my cousins who lived a few blocks away.

My idyllic world changed in 1973 when my dad accepted a job promotion as I entered seventh grade. This led to a move two hours north to Vancouver, Washington, replacing farm-town life with a city.

Striving to be accepted and find purpose, I involved myself in choir, drama and student government during the following years, winning class elections as a freshman and sophomore. In the fall of my junior year, I ran for office again, assuming I would win. However, when the results were announced at the end of a school day over the loudspeaker, I learned during geometry class that I'd lost.

Devastated by the news, I barely held my emotions in check while waiting for the last bell of the day. But before dismissal, my teacher asked me to stay after class.

I didn't know Mr. Marchbanks on a personal basis. My high school had over two thousand students, so students went from class to class having little personal connection to a teacher, unless you were interested, gifted or doing poorly.

When it came to geometry, I was neither gifted nor struggling. It just held little interest for me. I liked English, music and history, but not math. However, I did like this teacher. He made a difficult subject tolerable, expressing kindness and patience toward his students.

"Connie, you're probably upset about the results from the election today, aren't you?" he asked, while ushering me into his office cubicle after the final bell, as other teachers cleaned up papers and finished their workday around us.

I nodded silently, with tears threatening to spill over any minute. He looked at me with intense kindness and said, "Do you know you are not destined for only this?"

His question took me off guard.

"There is much more waiting for you. Right now all you see is the loss of this position. But I think you're being prepared for something in the future. In fact, I don't even see you staying here in Vancouver after graduation."

Although barely able to comprehend his meaning, I managed a glance at him as his words soaked into my receptive soul.

"God has something ahead for you that you don't know about right now. His hand is on you, and he wants to use you for his purposes. You may not even stay in the United States. He may call you to another country someday. Start listening to him, and know that what happened today is not the end of the world, but rather the beginning. God has plans for you—I'm sure of that."

I murmured a quick "thank you" and stumbled out of his office, trying to remember his words, but even more so, understand them.

Although I'd spent years in church as a child, God was not a part of my everyday life as a high school student. I never talked to him, never read the Bible, wasn't following him and didn't know he knew about me or had plans for my life.

Yet, if anyone had asked, I would have said I was a Christian. I was a good girl, obeyed my parents, got good grades and was kind to people. As far as I knew, that was the essence of living a Christian life.

So why did this teacher say that God's hand was on me? What was he talking about when he said I might not live in the United States? What prompted him to say these things to me?

I drove home that afternoon with his words ringing in my ears.

A few months later, a friend invited me to youth group at his church. I was shocked to find that Mr. Marchbanks, the teacher who had given those life-giving words, was the youth pastor.

Over the following months, he and his wife reached out to me often, speaking into my life about God and what they felt I was destined for. But I didn't have ears to hear.

Several months later, his wife invited me for a walk along the Columbia River. As we walked, she shared about what it means to give your life to Jesus and accept him as Savior. I felt uncomfortable and resisted making any commitment. I knew she cared, but feeling pressured, especially when she talked about joining their church, I turned her, and God, down.

At the beginning of my senior year, I won the office of student body president. I was the first girl to hold that office in the

history of the high school. I led fund-raisers for the community, planned school activities and implemented changes within the school throughout the year.

In October, the student government team and I planned Homecoming as part of our responsibilities. I volunteered to go downtown to buy the tiara for the one who would be newly crowned queen. Weeks later the former queen placed that tiara on my head.

In the winter, rather than play piano with the orchestra as I'd done the previous three years, I auditioned for a role in that year's musical production of *The Sound of Music* and was cast as Mother Superior. My parents had never heard me sing a solo until I sang onstage opening night.

My grades were nearly straight As. I took as many college preparatory classes as I could. I spoke at various functions, was elected to attend the American Legion Girls State and was the only girl from our high school chosen for all-state choir.

A few days before graduation, the principal announced the names of students graduating with honors in the top 5 percent (we didn't have valedictorians or salutatorians). My name was on the list.

On top of that, I was chosen for the top senior award that went to one boy and one girl out of our class of 630 students.

But days later as I walked out of the gymnasium after graduation, preparing to celebrate with family and friends, I had a bad feeling in the pit of my stomach. And had no idea why. All evening, during a party with my family at home, and later camping with friends, I felt utterly sad and empty, unable to shake the despairing thoughts in my head.

When I drove home the next morning, I entered the basement door of our family room. There on the mantel of the fireplace, my mom had placed all the awards I'd been given.

I sat down in front of them and cried.

Never had I felt emptier than I did that morning. As I hugged my knees to my chest and cried, I remember thinking, *What difference do all these things make now? I worked so hard ... and for what? When I go to college, no one will ever know who I was or what I did. No one will ask me what awards I won. Who will care that I held positions? Why did I think that mattered? What was the point of these past four years?*

Dragging through the next weeks, I felt depressed and out of sorts. Though outwardly I put on a happy face, I half-heartedly went to work each day feeling sad, lacking purpose and wishing something would change.

In mid-July a high school friend called. "Hey, Connie, this is Laurie. Are you free Saturday night?"

She invited me to Jesus Northwest, a Christian music festival at the county fairgrounds. Unfamiliar with Christian music, I didn't recognize the names of those she said would be there. Amy Grant would open the show, followed by Andraé Crouch & the Disciples.

Excited, but nervous, I drove to the Clark County Fairgrounds alone. I hadn't seen my friends since graduation and was feeling a hole in my heart for them, yet felt anxious about reconnecting. Would they see my sadness? Would they care? Would they reach out to help me? I hoped so.

Amy Grant was on stage at five o'clock, with people milling around the arena as she sang. I couldn't take my eyes off of her.

Something in her voice, words and demeanor spoke to me. I could tell she had something that I didn't have. And I wanted it, whatever it was.

Later in the evening, as Andraé Crouch & the Disciples sang, I felt a burning sensation from within. I was so captivated by the lyrics and music. Though in a sea of thousands, I felt as if I were the only one in the crowd. My heart beat wildly as I sensed a presence larger than myself, or anyone around me.

Near the end, Andraé's tone became serious. "There are people here tonight who think they know Jesus Christ. But let me tell you, going to church doesn't save you, nor does being good. The only way you'll know Jesus Christ is if you surrender your life to him: tell him you are a sinner, ask him to save you from your sins, put your faith and trust in him, take up his cross, deny yourself, say yes to following him for the rest of your life. THEN you'll know Jesus Christ.

"If you've been unsure of where you stand with God, let me tell you, tonight is your night! You can know Christ and the power that conquered the cross. You can know your sins are forgiven. You can know where you'll spend eternity. You can have eternal, abundant life—now, and forever.

"I'm going to lead you in a prayer right now. If you've never surrendered your life to Jesus Christ, I'm going to give you that opportunity. So would you bow your head and close your eyes, and repeat after me in the quiet of your own heart, a prayer that will lead you to assurance of salvation and set you apart as a follower of Christ."

With my heart beating wildly, I knew THIS was what I'd been missing and longing for!

I'd tried to be good, tried to follow the rules of living an upright life, and had sought to do good to others. And yet in that moment I realized that did nothing but lead me to sorrow and emptiness. Convicted of my sin and wanting desperately to change, I repented of my sin right there on the grassy field of the fairground. I believed in Jesus and his power of forgiveness and put my life in his hands.

When I did, it was everything my heart had longed for. Peace flowed through me and I felt deep rest in my soul. I said yes to Jesus that night, to all his plans and purposes, and gave my heart to following him wherever he would lead.

Later that night I pulled out my journal, sat on the floor in my room and wrote: "All this time I thought I was a Christian. I don't know how I missed what it is really about, but I didn't know YOU. I was living for myself, and I'm so sorry. Tonight, July 21, 1979, I put my faith in you, Jesus, and tell you that I will follow you and no one else. Help me to live the way YOU want me to live and go to the places where YOU want me to go. I promise to do whatever you ask."

And with those words, I became a true follower of Christ.

God's Promise
I delivered you from darkness into the kingdom of
my beloved son.
Colossians 1:12-13*

---

* God's Promises, quoted at the end of each chapter, are taken with permission from Barry Adams at 365Promises.com.

CHAPTER TWO

The Time Is Now

Four years of college passed quickly as I studied for a degree in education at Eastern Washington University. But most importantly, I grew as a believer in Jesus.

The culmination of all God had taught and shown me as he worked in my heart to lead me into a closer relationship with him came the night I stood at the Keith Green concert. With a newfound purpose and joy, I committed to following him wherever he led, even if it meant to the mission field.

But in my immediate future, I had other things to do. Although I went through my college graduation ceremony a few days after the concert, I still had to complete four months of student teaching, beginning in September. Choosing a different city from where I'd attended college, I boarded at a woman's house on the outskirts of Seattle and drove one hour to and from school each day.

During those long drives, I listened to a cassette tape a friend had made the previous summer while touring Western Europe with a group called Malachi. I cried as I listened to original songs written by the group's leader that talked about how it's your choice how you'll live—for God, or for yourself.

I'd had enough of living my own way and deeply longed to live a life of meaning, fully abandoned to God. But I didn't know what that meant for me personally. While I enjoyed my sixth-grade students that fall, I didn't have any sense of that being God's destiny for me. I wrestled day after day with what his plans for me were.

After finishing student teaching in early December, I moved back home with the hope and expectation of finding work and purpose. However, since Christmas was near, I put off my job search until the first of the year.

I'd found a church in Vancouver that I'd attended when home from college on weekends, as well as in summers. While I loved being part of the church body, it was a group of college-age friends there who especially challenged and encouraged me in my walk with God.

The first Sunday back at church after finishing student teaching, my best friend, Michelle Watson, greeted me at the door with these words, "Are you going to KC '83?"

Though I'd not heard of it before, I soon found that many in the college group had been planning and saving for Campus Crusade's college-age missions conference for months. However, with a five-hundred-dollar price tag, it was out of reach for me.

"I'm sure it's going to be fun for all of you. But there is no way that I can go," I told Michelle. "I'm completely broke, and

I can't ask my parents to pay after they've just put me through college. In fact, I've got to find a job after Christmas and start making money so I can move out and be responsible."

"You've GOT to go," she persisted. "It's going to be amazing, and you don't want to miss it."

But I knew I would.

After church while chatting with friends, I could see a young man, Nelson, standing off to the side waiting to talk to someone. We'd gone to high school together, but I didn't know him well so never expected it was me he was waiting for.

Yet as soon as I was free, he approached me. "Hey, Connie, could you stop by my house after church? I have something for you."

A half hour later, wondering what it could possibly be, I pulled up to his house and went to the door. He answered and stepped out onto the porch. "I was talking to Michelle today, and she told me that you should go to KC '83. I know this might sound strange, but I want to give this to you." He handed me an envelope.

"I've been working a job this year and started saving money for the conference months ago, and already paid for it back in the fall. But last week at church, a couple came to me and said they wanted to pay my way. When I told them I'd already paid, they gave me an envelope and said, 'Well, then you must know who this money is supposed to go to,' and they handed me this." Pointing to the envelope he said, "I think it's supposed to be for you."

In shock, I had no idea what to say.

"You can open it … if you want … there's five hundred dollars in it. If you go to the address of the travel agent I wrote on

the back of the envelope, you can book your ticket and pay for the conference. But tomorrow is the last day to do it, so you'll have to go right away."

After stammering some sort of thanks to Nelson, I drove home in awe at what had just happened. I didn't even fully know what the conference would be about! But it seemed obvious to me that God was at work to get me there. The next morning as I rushed over to Portland to book my ticket, I thanked him for the generosity of those who had made this possible.

The day after Christmas, I arrived in Kansas City with our college group and seventeen thousand other college students. Sitting in sessions with speakers like Josh McDowell and Elisabeth Elliot, we were challenged to give our lives to sharing the gospel and to consider lifetime missions work. "The time is now," they repeated over and over. "You can make a difference in this world by saying yes to God's call on your life."

Convicted and motivated by their challenge, I told the Lord I'd do whatever he wanted me to do. I was scared, yet excited at the thought of being part of his work somewhere in the world.

Walking alone through rows and rows of booths set up in the convention center, I talked with missionaries representing organizations and asked questions about what I could do. When I found the Campus Crusade jungle film team booth, I knew that was it. Nothing could be more difficult for me, but it seemed right to do the hardest thing possible for God. I thought that denying myself was what missions was all about.

After an hour with a representative, I signed the form to join a summer team who would show "The Jesus Film" in the

jungles of Argentina. I returned to the hotel, excited to tell Michelle about what I'd done.

I didn't get the reaction I expected.

"You can't do that! It's not how it works! You don't just sign up for the hardest thing you can think of," she said in dismay as we leaned against the wall in the hallway outside our room.

"You have to pray about these things, and look at the gifts he's given you, and then see how it fits together in his bigger plan."

My bubble was burst. I felt like crying. "But I want to do something for him. I want to follow him to the ends of the earth … well, at least for a summer. What else can I do? I don't know what I'm good at, or what I could possibly do for him."

Taking my hands in hers, she looked into my eyes and said, "You are SO gifted! Don't you know that? You've got music talent coming out your ears! Why don't you use that for him?"

"But that's too easy! I don't want to do something easy."

In earnest, she gently explained to me again, in greater detail, how one goes about following God.

"You pray, you talk to people, you ask God about your gifting, you look for things that match your passions and interests, you pray some more, you get godly counsel, you ask a lot of questions and do your research on what's available … and *then* you start to come to some conclusions," she said.

"Or … you let your best friend help you figure out where you're supposed to go. And I know just the ministry!" She grabbed my hands and said, "Let's go see if we can find Dave Patty."

I'd met Dave a few years earlier. He was a college student at Multnomah School of the Bible in Portland, Oregon, and an intern at my church in Vancouver.

I knew he led an evangelistic singing team on US military bases in Germany called Malachi, because Michelle had traveled with his group the previous summer. It was their songs I'd listened and cried to day after day while driving to the school where I did my student teaching. I'd heard that Dave's parents were missionaries and that he too planned to be a missionary when he finished Multnomah.

I wasn't sure I had much to offer his team and ministry. But I felt a sense of urgency to say yes to the Lord for one summer. So off we went in search of him to see if this was what I was supposed to do.

God's Promise
My plan for your future is filled with hope.
Jeremiah 29:11

CHAPTER THREE

Making a Decision

With seventeen thousand college students to navigate through, Michelle and I set off to find Dave.

Thinking he might be in the vicinity of the mission agency booths, we headed toward the convention hall where they were housed. But after an hour of searching and not finding him, we walked toward the exit. And there we encountered Elisabeth Elliot as she walked alone down the hall.

Not one to shy away from opportunity, Michelle approached her and began a conversation. "You have made *such* an impact on our lives," she began, gesturing to the two of us. "We've read all your books and admire the way you've lived your life for God. And we've loved hearing you speak! Your passion to follow God is so inspiring to us!"

Suddenly, over Elisabeth's shoulder, Michelle caught sight of Dave. "It was so nice meeting you, but we came to look for

someone and I see him over there! Thank you for talking with us." I don't think Elisabeth said one word to us, but being in her presence truly was inspiring.

We ran down the corridor and caught up to Dave and his friends just as they were leaving the building. "Dave! I'm so glad we found you!" Michelle said breathlessly. "We actually came looking for you because I wanted to talk to you about my friend Connie. You know her, right? She sings and plays the piano? I'm sure you've seen her at church. Well, I think she's a perfect fit for Malachi. Can she audition for this summer?"

The surprise was apparent on Dave's face. With his hand on the door, he politely responded, "Auditions are already closed. I'm really sorry. But it was nice to see you." He began to walk away.

Michelle persisted, "No, no … you don't understand, Connie is gifted and talented, and has a big heart for missions. She'd be perfect on the Malachi team next summer. Isn't there *some* way you could audition her, just as a favor to me?"

"Well, like I said, we've already finished all our auditions. But I guess if you want to contact David Schroeder when you get back to Portland, he could do an audition. I can't promise anything, but at least we'll have her information for the future."

I felt invisible during the interchange. And a little embarrassed. I didn't know much about the ministry of Malachi or about Dave, and it sounded like there wasn't an opening anyway. And did I really have a big heart for missions? This was all so new, but God *was* stirring something in my heart.

We said goodbye to him, and I breathed a sigh of relief.

For Michelle's sake, I was glad we'd found him. Now we could relax and enjoy the rest of the conference.

But once we returned to Portland, Michelle was on the phone to David, the other team leader for Malachi. Before I knew it, she'd arranged an audition in the practice rooms at Multnomah.

"They don't know it, but they want you," Michelle encouraged. With a best friend like that, who needs an agent? I love her to this day for pushing me into that audition.

David Schroeder met me outside the low white building that served as the music center for the Bible college. We headed into a tiny practice room with just a piano and a chair. He let me sit down, while he stood and interviewed me. "What kind of ministry experience have you had?" he asked.

"Well … not much," I answered honestly. "I've discipled a couple of girls during the summer and been a part of my college group."

"What's your philosophy of ministry?"

"My what?"

"What is your passion and vision for reaching the lost?"

Feeling completely out of my element, I fumbled for words that would make me sound as if I knew what I was talking about. I didn't sound very convincing to myself, and wondered what he was thinking.

"Okay … so let's do the musical part of the audition," David said after the interview.

Since I felt like I'd done horribly at answering the questions, somehow I relaxed and felt no pressure for the musical part of the audition. I knew they weren't going to take me.

He had me sight-read some music, sing and play the piano. We harmonized together as he recorded onto a little cassette recorder. He asked if I had a song I wanted to sing, which I didn't.

I left wondering again about going to the jungles of Argentina on the film team.

Michelle called that evening to find out how the interview and audition had gone. I hardly had the heart to tell her that it hadn't gone well. I was sad to disappoint her. "They'll call in a few weeks if they're interested," I said, making it sound like there was a chance. But I knew they wouldn't call.

Days later I received a call, but it wasn't from Dave. Rather it was from the Evergreen District substitute teacher's administrator. I'd been substitute teaching in various schools since the first of the year.

"Hi, Miss France. I'm calling to ask if you'd be interested in a long-term sub job? We've got a teacher who was sadly just diagnosed with a brain tumor, and she'll be out for the rest of the school year. We don't have many on our sub list who are interested in teaching full-time, but I thought of you since you're fresh out of college, that maybe you'd be interested in getting the experience.

"It's a sixth-grade class at Mill Plain Elementary. There's a teaching team of two other teachers who would work with you and help with lesson plans. They team-teach some subjects, so you wouldn't be completely on your own. And this happens to be the smallest class of the three, just twenty-four students."

Just twenty-four? I'd be responsible for twenty-four students? They'd let me do that? Scared to death, but knowing that this was

an opportunity that couldn't be passed up, I gulped and said yes. Then asked when I should be there.

"Well, if you could start tomorrow, it would be helpful. Otherwise I'll have to put a sub in there for a few days, and then you'd take over. I think it'd be better if you got started right away. It'd be less disruptive for the kids that way."

Hanging up the phone, I put my head in my hands. What had I just signed up for?

Nervously, I pulled into the parking lot of Mill Plain Elementary the next morning. I didn't want to be there! The introvert side of me felt like heading for my turtle shell, and I truly wondered about the sanity of saying yes to this job.

However, the night before as I'd prayed about it, the Lord brought to mind the yet-unseen faces of the kids who were impacted by this series of events. They were going to be confused and disoriented with their teacher leaving so suddenly. Could I be a help to them?

And if the Lord led me to take the job, wouldn't he be there as I walked through the front doors, and help me to do what he wanted?

With a deep breath and a whispered prayer for his presence, I entered the classroom.

In hindsight, I don't know if I was the one they should have hired to teach. But I'm confident I was the one to hire to love on those kids. And love I did.

We had our struggles; there were fights on the playground, disrespectful voices in the classroom, undone homework and a teacher who barely knew how to teach. But over the next four

months, we bonded in a way I wouldn't have thought possible. I really loved those kids.

And I was grateful for the other two, much more experienced sixth-grade teachers who took a fledgling under their wings and made me successful.

Toward the end of February, I was at home in the evening working on lesson plans. I heard the phone ring and then I heard my mom call, "Connie, there's someone on the phone!"

"Hello? This is Connie."

"Connie, it's Dave Patty."

Why is he calling me?

With silence on my end, since I wasn't sure what to say, he continued, "I don't know if you remember me. We met at KC '83?"

"Oh, yes … of course, yes … I know you. Sorry, I was just startled to hear from you."

"Well, I'm calling to ask if you'd consider praying about being on Malachi this summer."

Is he kidding? "Um … really? I didn't actually think … well, you know … really, you want me on your team?"

"Well, I'd like you to pray about it. If God confirms that you're to spend the summer with us, yes, I'd like you on my team."

Gulp. I was shocked. How had this happened? I managed to get out a few intelligent questions, but I was shaking so badly I could hardly think. As soon as we hung up, I made a phone call.

"Michelle, you'll never guess who just called me!"

"Dave Patty?" she asked.

"What? How did you know?" I nearly shouted into the phone.

She laughed. "I didn't know he was going to call today, but I *did* think he'd call you."

"You did? I never really told you how badly the audition went. How could you think he'd want me on his team?"

After a slight pause she answered, "Oh, because I think you're going to marry him."

Silence hung over the phone line.

I finally managed to mutter in frustration, "Why on earth would you say something like that?"

"Oh, come on, you know I'm just teasing. But I do think he'll like you. Who wouldn't?"

"Okay … well, can we leave that subject and talk about whether or not I should do this?" I asked.

"Well, *you* can talk about it. But I already know what's going to happen."

Grrrrr. It's hard when your best friend seems to know the future and you don't.

We talked over some of the details I'd need to consider as I prayed: raising money, leaving my students early, serving for a summer with people I didn't know. It felt overwhelming. But as I sat in my room that night, the thought occurred to me, *Why wouldn't I do this?*

The Bible is clear about going and making disciples.

The circumstances leading up to this felt like the leading of the Spirit, not just coincidences.

I definitely had the encouragement of godly people whom I trusted and respected.

And, if I believe God is truly in control of all things, then couldn't I trust that he would take care of the details that felt overwhelming?

I also remembered the words of my teacher who planted the seed that God wants to use me for his purposes.

I called Dave the next day and told him yes.

God's Promise
I am at work in your life through the desires of your heart.
Philippians 2:13

CHAPTER FOUR

A Summer Awakening

A s I taught my class of twenty-four sixth-graders, I now had the added task of raising support for a summer with Malachi. This was a daunting task.

Surprisingly, the funds to cover my summer in Europe came within a few months. I had only written a letter, shared it in person with a few people and given a presentation at church. I am so thankful for those people who took a risk on sending an inexperienced young woman to the mission field for a summer.

During the months before leaving, I connected through letters and phone calls with the other three girls who would be on the team that summer: Laura Larrabee, Jerri Miller and Joyce Patty, Dave's older sister. We planned our outfits: two matching dresses, as well as matching T-shirts for everyone. Yes, this was the '80s, and we had to match.

Teaching continued to go smoothly, and I was excited about the prospect of coming back to teach there in the fall, if not in

a full-time position, at least as a favorite sub. I knew the ins and outs of the school, enjoyed the kids and liked my fellow teachers.

On a sunny day in late May, my parents drove me to Multnomah Bible College to meet up with a carload driving to Denver, where we would spend three weeks in training before leaving for Germany.

I had talked to Jerri on the phone, but this was the first time I had met her in person. We found an instant kinship and bond. Climbing into the backseat, we spent well over half of the twenty-four hours en route to Denver sharing our hearts with each other.

The ride went by quickly, and before I knew it we were pulling up in front of Dave's aunt and uncle's house, which would be our home base during the weeks of training.

Over the next three weeks, the eight of us bonded as a team. Although we'd be divided up into groups of four during most of the summer, we spent many hours together learning music and drama, and even produced a recording to sell while in Europe.

The longer I was with those seven people, the more comfortable I became. I liked who they were. I loved their hearts for God. And I loved how it made me want to follow even harder after him myself. They began to feel like family.

As the plane lifted off for my first overseas flight, I breathed a sigh of relief, knowing I was in the right place that God had chosen for me. When we landed in Frankfurt the next morning, I wanted to pinch myself! Never in my wildest imagination had I seen myself coming to Germany. Ever.

And I wasn't there as a tourist, but as a missionary.

Dave's dad, Dick Patty, a missionary with Overseas Christian Servicemen's Center in Germany, picked us up at the airport. Knowing it was the first time in Europe for a few of us, he drove us into Ladenburg, a delightful German village. I felt like I was in a fairy tale: timbered houses; shuttered windows; colorful flower boxes; spired cathedrals; narrow, cobblestoned streets and the sound of the German language everywhere.

I sat in the backseat, gazing out at the sights, praising God for allowing me to have this special summer opportunity to serve him.

We settled in at the Patty house in St. Leon-Rot, which would be our home base for the summer. Once over jet lag, we began spending our days praying for the summer, talking about the schedule and planning for the various ministry opportunities we'd have throughout the summer.

Our first event was an annual camping trip in Lauterbrunnen, Switzerland, for military personnel and their families who were involved in OCSC hospitality houses.

"Switzerland? We're going to Switzerland?" I asked excitedly. "I didn't know the American military had bases there!"

They don't.

But that says how completely green I was about what I'd signed up for. Or rather, the path God had asked me to follow him on. I knew so little about missions, and even less about the American military we would be serving.

The camping trip was a gathering of military families who served in Germany, put together by OCSC hospitality house directors. Everyone brought their own tents and cooking supplies,

and could spend their days taking outings in the Alps. But each evening in the campground, there was Bible teaching, worship, games and fellowship for the whole group.

Malachi provided worship and led games, along with giving concerts of our newly prepared music. I was ecstatic about being there. Switzerland had long been on my list of "wish I could see" places, although I'd never actually considered how or when I'd ever go. But here it was, the first place on the list of Malachi events for the summer.

The first night there, we gave a concert underneath the rush of the waterfall in the Jungfrau Camping campground, in a canyon lined with towering Alps above us. It was a breathtaking scene.

The concerts were more than just music. We sang songs, performed skits and gave testimonies.

Having never done anything like this before, I was scared about speaking in front of an audience; afraid I wouldn't have anything to say, I spent a lot of time trying to think of significant words to share each night.

One evening, before a concert, David Schroeder asked me to take a walk.

As we headed over to a large rock at the edge of the campground to sit down, I was afraid of what he was going to say to me. Did he think it was a mistake bringing me on the team? Was I doing something wrong? Everything in me wanted to run and hide, but I stoically followed him to the rock.

"Hey, I just want to tell you, you're doing a really great job for your first time of being with Malachi," David kindly began as we sat down. "I know it's a lot to take in, and maybe is hard

because some of us have been doing this for a few years. You might be feeling a little intimidated," he continued.

He was right about that.

"But here's the thing. What we really want is for you to grow and mature in your walk with God, and this is a great, safe environment to do that. You don't have to have all the right answers, or do everything perfectly. Just share honestly, be vulnerable and let God lead you, rather than trying to do it for him."

Gulp. That wasn't what I expected.

I was so afraid of all of them seeing through me, and finding out how I was really feeling about being there: scared, nervous, faithless, wondering why I was there. But now he was telling me it was okay to be vulnerable. I started to cry.

"I don't know how to be vulnerable, and I don't know if I have anything significant to say," I tearfully said to him, not even able to look up.

"Well, you're being vulnerable right now!" he replied. "Speaking out of your insecurity is better than trying to make it look like you know what you're doing. You don't. And that's okay. We're going to love you and help you through this. But you've got to let us in and give us a chance to speak into your life. You don't have to have it all together. That's not the end goal."

He asked if he could pray with me, and then left me on the rock for time to compose myself, and more importantly, to pray and ask God to help me open up, be vulnerable and let him lead me.

I was quiet the rest of the evening. They didn't ask me to speak during the concert that night, for which I was grateful.

But there was plenty going on inside me. I longed to emerge and be myself, yet was so afraid that they wouldn't like me or accept me if I opened up. But David had given an invitation to do just that.

So I committed once again to saying yes to whatever the Lord asked of me, and told him that any time he prompted me to speak my true heart, I would, even if it felt scary and made me feel vulnerable. I committed to trust in him and not lean on my own understanding, but rather let him guide me.

It was not easy. I'd spent a lot of years hiding my true feelings of insecurity and uncertainty, so it was hard to change that pattern. But with baby steps, I attempted to.

We left Switzerland a few days later and drove to Spain, the next place of ministry, at the Rota Naval Base.

Little did I know what I was about to encounter.

God's Promise
Trust in me with all your heart and I will guide you.
Proverbs 3:5-6

CHAPTER FIVE — Change of Plans

A fter two and a half days of driving, and a lot of conversation with my three teammates, we arrived at the Victory Villa hospitality house in Rota, Spain.

During those two days of travel, I began to open my heart to my teammates, Dave, Steve and Laura, entrusting them with parts of my story, thoughts and feelings. While it would take me time to live in full openness and vulnerability, I was off to a good start.

It was after 10 p.m. when we arrived at the back door of the Villa, everyone tired from our long journey. Set on the edge of a cliff overlooking the sandy beach of Rota, this old Spanish home provided a place for Navy men and women to fellowship, have Bible studies, get a home-cooked meal, be discipled and even spend the night if they wanted.

The directors, Bill and Jeannette Kramer, met us under the lone light bulb at the back door on that warm summer evening.

Opening the creaky screen door, they welcomed us in, told us where our rooms were and to go ahead and get settled for the night.

Except for me.

"Connie, would you mind staying here for a bit?" Bill inquired as he ushered me over to their small kitchen table while Jeannette poured glasses of water for the three of us.

Watching my teammates go through the door, leaving me in the company of people I'd never met, I felt nervous. Why were they asking me to stay? The three of us sat facing one another at the table, me with a quizzical look on my face.

"You're a schoolteacher, is that right?" Bill asked.

"Yes," I hesitantly answered. "I finished my student teaching this past December, and then subbed for a few months …" I didn't know how to go on from there.

Bill picked up the loose end and continued, "Jeannette and I have a son, Jeffrey—he's sleeping now and you'll meet him tomorrow. He just finished first grade, being homeschooled by Jeannette. But as we evaluated how this first year went, we feel like it would be better for him to have a teacher other than his mom. We're wondering if you'd consider coming here to live and teach next year?"

What? I looked at them in wide-eyed shock. I couldn't get one word to come out of my mouth. My first night in Spain and I was being asked to come and live here. *For a year?*

This was definitely not what I had in mind when I committed to saying yes to the Lord, asking him to deepen my walk with him and help me be more open and vulnerable with others.

"I know this probably comes as a shock, but we just wanted to get it right out in the open tonight so that you have time to think and pray about it, get to know Jeffrey and us, and see if this is what God might have ahead for you," Bill kindly explained.

Since I still didn't know what to say, Bill finished with, "I don't know what you're thinking right now, but I just want to ask one question: Why wouldn't you come?"

I couldn't believe he asked me the same question I'd asked myself months earlier when Dave called to invite me to serve with Malachi for the summer. Pondering that thought, wondering what God was doing, I went to join Laura in our room for the night.

The next days were a blur. I remember bits and pieces of ministering to teenagers on the Navy base, and of military personnel coming to the Villa for a concert. But most of my thoughts were consumed with *What should I do?*

Bill offered to let me call my parents and talk it over with them, once I told them I was at least open to exploring the option. This was no small offer, as phone calls to the States in those days were more than two dollars per minute. But Bill and Jeannette were willing to pay that cost to help me overcome one of the hurdles that I'd expressed: What would my parents say?

Over the crackling of a very long distance phone call, I reached my mom and dad in Washington. After giving them a quick rundown on the events that had taken place, I asked, "What do you think?"

Mom replied first. "When we waved you off from the parking lot at Multnomah, I turned to Dad and said, 'I don't think she's coming back.' I didn't mean that as in, you'll never come to

visit. I meant that this was your calling, your destiny, and that you'd probably continue on this road for the rest of your life."

"So," my dad picked up the thought, "if this is something you feel that God is leading you toward, and that in order to follow him you need to do it, we are fully supportive."

Their unwavering support brought tears to my eyes.

We talked for a few minutes longer, and then I hung up the phone, thankful for such unselfish parents. Though it meant letting me go, they wished for me to do what was right in God's eyes. That was a very precious gift.

But I still didn't know what to do.

Our last day in Rota, we had the afternoon free. The four of us went down to a resort area on the beach to enjoy the sun, play Frisbee and swim. Dave and I ended up going out into the water and riding the waves together for an hour, buoyant in the salty sea.

"So are you thinking about coming back to Rota or not?" Dave asked as we bobbed up and down in the waves, looking back toward shore.

"I don't know. I'm actually kind of confused about it all," I answered. And that was the truth. But I couldn't actually tell him the whole story.

I was having feelings for him. And I knew that he was going to be staying in Europe to begin his role as director of a new ministry that had developed out of Malachi. He wanted to do long-term discipleship with the teenagers who were coming to Christ, and planned to start Malachi Ministries which would place youth workers in military chapels. He was also going to study Spanish in Madrid for a few months.

I didn't want my decision to be based on anything other than pure motives. But how to do that when I knew his plans, and how those could be connected to mine?

Later that afternoon I walked in the gardens of the Villa, praying and asking God for some kind of sign. What he gave was better than that.

He replayed in my mind all the events of the past year: the Keith Green concert; KC '83; being invited to Malachi; substitute teaching for four months and gaining valuable experience. I remembered the talk in Lauterbrunnen with David, and my subsequent commitment and prayer to the Lord, asking him to deepen me and make me more open and vulnerable.

I had no debt and no bills. I didn't have a job waiting for me. I'd been trained as a teacher. I knew I'd been called to something back at the Keith Green concert. I was starting to feel the "real me" come alive, and I liked that. Bill and Jeannette even said they'd help me financially, though they hoped I would be able to raise some support. Finances didn't seem to be a deterrent to my coming there.

What I did have back at home was a boyfriend.

But my conflicting feelings for Dave (though unnoticed and unreciprocated by him) told me that something was going on in my heart in regard to that relationship, and that I would need to think and pray about it.

Everything else seemed to be pointing in the direction of Spain and teaching school for one little boy. So before we left the next day, I told Bill and Jeannette that I'd come back in September and stay for a school year.

Looking back, this was the most pivotal decision I'd made in my life, aside from putting my faith in Jesus at the concert in the summer of 1979.

It was also the most courageous move I'd ever made to follow God. Up until then, I'd made no decisions that had the potential for long-lasting impact in my life. But this decision was different. Oh, so very different.

It would set a course for a life that would never return to the old way. God was orchestrating events in my life that were beyond my comprehension at the time. And yet, there was a certain sense of peace in knowing that all that had occurred up until this point seemed to be fitting together into something of value and worth. And I wanted that in my life.

As I drove away from the Villa with my teammates, I couldn't help but think about all that would happen in my life during the school year I would spend there.

During the two-day drive back from Spain, I felt like a light switch had turned on and that I was really alive for the first time in my life.

When the day of my departure arrived several weeks later, I didn't want the summer to end. So much had happened in my life among these people, and I wished it could continue. The spiritual growth that had taken place in me had happened in their presence, and I was nervous that it was just temporary and wouldn't "stick" when I left them.

On my twenty-third birthday, I found myself at the Frankfurt International Airport, saying goodbye to people who now felt like family. As we stood in the terminal, we made promises to see one another in the fall if at all possible. Dave, David, Joyce

and Laura were all staying for a new segment of Malachi's ministry: traveling into specific military communities on a weekly basis to do discipleship groups with high school students. On the weekends they would continue to give concerts, finishing in December.

I told them I would try to save money so that I could come up to see them in the fall. And with that we gave last hugs and said our goodbyes.

Dave was the last one I hugged. It wasn't on purpose, just the way it worked out. But when we moved in for the hug, it was like an electric shock went through me. We lingered in the hug longer than I had with anyone else, and I realized I didn't want to leave *him*. But I pulled away and walked to my gate with tears falling down my face. As I made my way onto the airplane and found my seat where I would sit for the next ten hours, I pondered all that had happened in me that summer.

Many people say short-term missions is not a good investment of money, that you could take the same amount of dollars it takes to send someone overseas and use that to do something in the country they were going to go minister in. But after a life-changing summer, I saw the value in it. Yes, missions is about reaching the lost for Christ. But it's also about transformation in the lives of those bringing the good news.

I was reborn during those three pivotal months. I went a naïve, spiritually immature girl, and blossomed into a growing, vibrant, faith-filled young woman. The person flying back to the US on that plane was not the same girl who had flown from the US just months earlier.

The months of actively sharing my faith, of studying God's Word daily with my teammates, of praying for and seeing God's movement in the lives of teenagers and military personnel, was more than I ever expected. It was positively exhilarating. And I wanted more of it.

I didn't know what was ahead in Spain, but I felt sure of God's leading, and had a deepening desire to follow him to this new place. If these months of ministry had been so formational in my life, I wondered what nine months in Spain would be like? I couldn't wait to get back there.

God's Promise
I will reward those who diligently seek me with a heart of faith.
Hebrews 11:6

CHAPTER SIX
Life in Spain

My two weeks at home sped by.

While I'd been gone for the summer, my Grandpa France had unexpectedly passed away. So I visited and grieved with my grandma. I spent time with my family. I hung out with Michelle and my college youth group friends.

And I tried to break up with my boyfriend.

During the summer I'd already written to him telling about the opportunity to teach Jeffrey in Spain. Since that letter, the opportunity had grown into a one-room schoolhouse with three students. I'd have a first-, second- and sixth-grader, all at one time.

He was genuinely excited for me and told me I should accept this opportunity since it seemed clear God was leading me toward it. But back at home, when I brought up the fact that I was uncertain about our relationship and my feelings for him, he told me not to worry and that we'd figure out our future when I returned the next spring. I wasn't sure about that, but accepted it and left for Spain still his girlfriend.

My parents drove me to Seattle to catch my flight on the charter airline Sabena based in Belgium. It had been the cheapest flight I could find. Being new to air travel, I didn't fully understand when they told me there would be an overnight in Amsterdam, but was glad to know they'd booked me into a hotel. I assumed someone would be at the airport to meet me and take me there.

Getting on that flight was much harder than when I had first left my parents in the Multnomah parking lot. This felt permanent, even though I'd only committed to teach for a school year. But somehow, I knew this was a turning point and that things would never be the same from that point on.

I cried for an hour after we took off.

The flight landed in Amsterdam in the late afternoon, and when I came out into the main concourse of the airport I looked for someone to meet me. Not finding anyone, I asked about my hotel at the information desk and learned that it was a 45-minute bus ride away, in the center of Amsterdam.

With nothing more than an address, I climbed on the bus with my carry-on, hoping somehow I'd find my way to the hotel. Very few people spoke English, and I had a hard time finding someone on the bus to help me. I ended up riding the bus to the end of the line, hoping against hope that I'd find my way from there.

Let off in front of the train station, I went from person to person, showing them the address and trying to find someone who knew which direction to point me in. I ended up in a butcher shop with a man who didn't speak English, but who drew out directions for me, complete with store diagrams of how many buildings it would be before I made a turn.

I walked as far as I could, and then lost my way. It was after 6 p.m. by this time, and shops were closing, so there was no one else to point me in the right direction. I stood in the middle of a small street, with tall brownstones on either side, and cried out to the Lord, "Show me what to do."

Then I looked up and saw the name of the hotel; or rather, the name of a quaint boardinghouse.

Sabena had booked me into a small *pensioen*, as it was called in Dutch. Run by an order of nuns, there were tiny rooms with a sink and a shower, with not even a curtain to partition off the spray of water into the room. I didn't care at that point. I laid down on the stiff, twin-size bed and fell fast asleep for three hours.

By the time I woke up, I knew I'd missed the dinner they'd prepared. But when I looked out the window at the dark streets, and only a few lighted houses, I realized there was probably nowhere for me to get something to eat. So I set an alarm and went back to sleep, hungry.

Nervous that I'd somehow not be able to find my way back to the airport, I woke up before my alarm. Tentatively, I made my way downstairs to the room where breakfast was being served, to get something to satisfy my growling stomach. I also hoped to find someone who could help me get back to the airport for my afternoon flight to Spain.

As I stood trying to communicate with the nun at the desk, a young woman came up behind me and asked with a Texas accent if I needed help. "I hear you need to get to the Amsterdam airport. I can take you there if you'd like," she said with her warm Texas drawl. Are there angels in Texas? I think she was one!

I asked when she could leave, and she said as soon as I needed to. While I knew I'd sit in the airport and wait for several hours, I was anxious to get there. So I hurried to my room, gathered my things and met her in the entryway. How good of God to send her, whomever she was, to help me find my way back to the airport.

Hours later, my flight to Malaga, Spain, took off, and I was on my way to the final destination.

Bill and Jeannette had driven nearly four hours to the airport to pick me up. While it was a long day for them, they were still cheery and chatty as we made our way back to Rota, traveling down close to Gibraltar, and up through the mountains over to Jerez, and finally to the Villa, on the outskirts of Rota.

They'd rented an apartment for me, half a block from the Villa, so took me there for my first night in the country. The three-bedroom apartment felt huge as I rattled around in there that first night, trying to get my bearings. It overlooked the ocean, and was steps away from the small summer apartment the three sets of parents had rented for our schoolroom.

The next morning I woke up to bright sunshine, and homemade granola and yogurt Jeannette had left for me. There was definitely a feeling of "Toto, we're not in Kansas anymore," as I looked out at the Rota bay, shimmering in the distance, and felt the heat of the day already rising even though it was September. I'd have a lot to learn here.

I'd taken Spanish from elementary school through high school, so the language didn't scare me. I was by no means proficient in it, but it sounded familiar, even though it was Castilian

Spanish, not the type I had learned. But somehow I knew I'd get by.

They gave me my first week to get oriented, figure out how to work everything in my apartment, learn how to buy groceries and get myself around town. They showed me the "chicken man" downtown, who made a divine grilled chicken over open coals for just a couple of dollars (or *pesetas*, as was the currency in Spain then).

I didn't have a car, but they had an extra one at the Villa for me to drive when needed. They pointed me in the right direction, and I headed to Jerez, a half-hour away, where Jeannette told me there was *Hipercor*, a huge grocery store where she said I could find anything.

I don't remember what else I came home with that first day, but I know for sure it was Fritos and Coke, familiar items that made me feel a little less homesick. It's odd, but I've never seen Fritos in Europe since, and I've always liked to think they were there just for me that year.

The first day of school arrived, and I was nervously excited to get going. Nervous because I'd never had full rein of teaching, but excited to meet my three kids and begin to build relationships with them. I'd prepared bulletin boards and signs welcoming them, as well as arranged desks and chairs, and a special reading area for them. With two rooms in the apartment, and a rather dilapidated, but working bathroom, I was ready for business!

Jeffrey, Morgan and Kristin were right on time Monday morning, along with their parents, as we'd decided to have an "opening ceremony" to get started.

Jeffrey was Bill and Jeannette's seven-year-old son. Towheaded and full of energy, he was excited to be in a real classroom for the first time.

Morgan, the daughter of a naval officer, was my first-grader. While she could've enrolled in the school on base (which wasn't available to Jeffrey because neither parent was military), her parents decided to give her a more personal first year of school after they heard that I was coming to teach.

Kristin was twelve, and in sixth grade that year. Her parents were missionaries, involved in planting a Spanish-speaking church in Rota. They spoke excellent Spanish and were often my translators. Vibrant and in love with Jesus, they were also a great source of spiritual encouragement.

My student-teaching in Washington had been with sixth-graders. So I felt at home with Kristin, and knew how to relate to and motivate her, being both teacher and friend to her that year. We memorized Scripture together, spent recesses talking while Morgan and Jeffrey played and developed a sweet friendship.

But as much as I enjoyed teaching my three students, I found the greatest joy in working with teenagers on the military base that year. Becoming a volunteer at weekly youth group meetings, I spent my free time hanging out with high-schoolers and leading Bible studies for the girls. As the months passed by, I could feel myself being drawn to full-time work with youth, rather than life as a teacher.

It also became apparent that other changes were in order. I broke up with my boyfriend that fall, and applied for the graduate program at Multnomah School of the Bible.

In January, I flew with Bill and Jeannette to the annual OCSC missionary conference in Beatenberg, Switzerland, at the Bibelheim. Perched on the side of a snow-covered mountain, overlooking Lake Thun and the Alps, it was a magnificent place to meet with God and the perfect setting for a conference.

The reunion with my former teammates was a happy one. Laura and Joyce were anxious to catch up and hear everything about me, and I looked forward to hearing their stories as well. Sitting on thick feather comforters draped over beautiful, wooden Swiss sleigh beds, we happily shared our hearts with one another.

After dinner, missionaries shared testimonies and stories about people coming to Christ, and spoke genuinely about struggles. I appreciated their honesty and felt deeply at home with them.

After the evening program I saw Dave waiting, but didn't know why. I continued on in conversation with the girls.

I had done a lot of thinking about him in the months since I'd seen him, and especially since I'd broken up with my boyfriend. I realized that I had feelings for Dave, but didn't feel right about expressing them to him. With my plan to return to the States for Bible school after finishing the school year with my kids, it seemed best to move on from those feelings.

When there was a break in our conversation, Dave stepped in and said, "Hey, Connie, I'd love to hear about those kids you're teaching and what you're learning these days. Do you want to go get tea over in the main building?"

That evening we laughed and joked, reminiscing about the past summer and telling stories about what had been happening

in our lives since then. There was a lot to catch up on. He told me how the first wave of discipleship groups had gone, and how the two new Malachi ministries on bases in Mannheim and Stuttgart were going. He was excited about what God was doing, and I was genuinely happy to hear about it all.

Then he suddenly turned the conversation and asked, "So I heard about your breakup. How are you doing with that?"

It was such a gentle question, and I felt brotherly love and protection from him as I shared how I'd come to that decision. I told him everything—except for how I felt about him.

We parted ways, and I felt settled in my heart that I'd made the right decision not to tell him.

I didn't see him again until after the evening program the following night. This time when he approached me, there was awkwardness between us.

"I was just wondering … are you doing anything right now?" he asked, trying to be casual, yet I could see he was uncomfortable.

"No … what were you thinking?" I tentatively asked.

"Well … would you have time to talk … maybe get tea again? I mean, if you have time or if you want to. No pressure if you don't …" he trailed off.

I spared him any further agony and said, "Sure, I'd love to." And off we went to the tearoom again.

It was the same room, but a very different atmosphere between us.

We sat in silence over our cups of tea, my knees literally knocking under the table, and my teeth threatening to chatter at any moment.

What was going on?

We tried to make small talk, but it wasn't working. Finally, Dave took a breath and started in, "You're probably wondering why I asked you here?"

I nodded, glancing up at him, as I didn't trust my voice to speak at that moment.

"Well, last night I got together with you because I genuinely wanted to hear about how you were doing. But I also wanted to know where you were really at with your boyfriend, well, I mean your ex-boyfriend. I had to know if it was really over. Do you know what I'm talking about?"

Yikes. Did I?

"When you left in August, and we hugged goodbye, I went back to St. Leon and talked to David about you. See, I realized that I liked you. But I knew I couldn't do anything about it since you were still dating. That would've been dishonorable. So I just prayed and put you in God's hands and waited to see if he'd do anything about what I was feeling.

"I've been thinking since last night, after you told me how you were doing, that I'd like to ask you a question. What would you think ... about getting to know each other better?"

Stunned, I sat in happy silence. What could I say to that?

"Well," I ventured, "I'd actually like that. A lot." And I smiled.

All the tension broke at that point, and we just started laughing, talking long into the evening. Not about us or about anything in the future, just the sort of talking we'd done in the summer: honest, relaxed, open. I felt like I could completely be myself, and he was fully himself. It was a relief to relate this way to each other.

The next day he invited me to go with him on a famous 10-kilometer sled run not far from Beatenberg. A bus came to pick everyone up and load in the sleds for the trip. When I saw Dave put just one sled in, I honestly asked, "What will I use on the sled run?"

His eyes twinkled, and he replied, "You're on a sled with me!"

And so we headed off on our first date. With Dave behind me, I sat in front on our little Swiss sled, hanging on for all I was worth as we careened down the snowy road.

At one point I tried to put out my legs to help slow us down, but he was quick to say, "You can trust me. Just hang on and you'll be okay."

Those were very good words for where we were headed.

God's Promise
You can trust in me, for I am your strength and your song.
Isaiah 12:2

CHAPTER SEVEN

T he following months passed quickly.

News arrived of my acceptance into Multnomah's graduate program. Days were full of teaching the kids, and I continued on with youth group activities as winter turned into spring. Dave and I saw each other several times while he studied Spanish in Madrid, and our friendship deepened.

That summer I spent traveling with Malachi again, though Dave was not there. Instead he was in the States raising support to serve full time with Malachi. He arrived in Germany a few days before I left for the States to begin graduate school.

It had actually been a hard summer in regard to our relationship. There were letters and occasional cassette tapes, but I felt something missing between us. Dave felt distant, and I couldn't tell how he was feeling about me, about our future or us. Our letters consisted of what we were doing, rather than what was going on in our hearts and souls.

After saying goodbye in Frankfurt, the plane ride back to Portland, Oregon, was a somber one, as I wasn't sure where our relationship was headed.

Classes at Multnomah started soon after I returned. Laura, my teammate the first summer with Malachi, had also decided to attend the grad program, so we moved into a house and shared a bedroom that year. She was my oasis of comfort in those days, willing to lend an ear and listen to my heart cries.

Needing a job, I applied first for something on campus, hoping I would be able to save on gas money by working close by. Although jobs were at a premium, I was offered one in housekeeping, and happily took it.

For ten hours a week, my job was to clean all the offices in the administration building at the end of each workday. It meant getting a late meal in the cafeteria, if I even made it there in time. But happy to have a job, I eagerly set about cleaning after five o'clock each day, when all the professors, secretaries and administrators had gone home.

There was always a light on at the end of one hall, so I waited to clean there last. But more times than not, the light was still on by the time I reached that office, so I would knock before entering and then try to clean around the woman still working in there.

Dr. Pam Reeve had been the dean of women for years at Multnomah. She was also a professor, an author and conference speaker, and many sought her out for her words of wisdom and biblical insight.

I met her while taking out her trash.

For days, I tiptoed around her while cleaning, until one day she invited me to sit down and asked me who I was, and why I was at Multnomah. I missed dinner that night. And I guess she did too. We talked until late in the evening as I shared my story, and she told me hers.

When she heard I was dating Dave, her eyes lit up and twinkled in a way that she was well known for. She knew Dave from his years studying at Multnomah and clapped her hands together like a schoolgirl when she heard we were dating.

In her distinct voice that I can hear to this day, she said, "Oh, how grand is that! He's a dandy one, that Dave! That's just wonderful news to hear. He needs a girl like you. Don't let him push you away. He's got a tough exterior, but there's a soft heart in there somewhere!"

Letters from Dave continued that fall, but were empty of emotion. After much soul-searching, and talks with Pam and other friends, I felt it was time to end our relationship. Not because I didn't love him, but because I didn't sense that he loved me. It was a painful decision. But one I knew the Lord was asking me to make.

I trudged to the post office the next morning, package in hand with a cassette tape I'd made expressing my heart. It took every ounce of courage and will to hand over that package and send it on its way to Germany.

Ten excruciating days passed as that package made its way over the ocean to St. Leon and into his hands. I prayed like I'd never prayed before. Over and over, I gave Dave into the Lord's hands, and told him I would stay true to following only him. As best as I could, I set my gaze on the Lord and moved on, waiting for the day when my heart would stop aching.

Laura was the epitome of a best friend during those days. No matter that we had assignments due. No matter that we had pages and pages of reading in front of us. No matter that she was supposed to be meeting with other girls as part of her responsibility for being the resident assistant in our house. She spent countless hours in our room, crying and praying with me, believing that God would get me through this.

One early morning as we were getting ready for classes, the shared phone for all the apartments rang in the stairway. Laura went to answer it.

I heard her quick footsteps as she rushed back to our room, her voice calling out in a loud whisper, "CONNIE! It's Dave! He wants to talk to you."

My heart sunk. I didn't have anything else to say to him. And I was afraid to hear his words of "Okay, it's over. I just wanted to say goodbye."

But with Laura's urgings, I cautiously stepped into the hall and put the receiver to my ear.

"Hi, this is Connie …"

"Connie … it's Dave. Can you talk?"

With a lump in my throat, and tears in my eyes, I sighed and told him yes.

"Listen. I just got your cassette. It came in the mail today, so as I left for Heidelberg, I put it in to listen to while I drove. But before I even made it to the autobahn, I knew something wasn't right, so I turned around and headed back home and listened to the whole thing.

"You're right," he said earnestly, "I haven't been loving you, but I want to learn how. You have the right problem, but the

wrong solution. There is another one. Would you give me a second chance?"

I was hesitant. Not because I didn't still love him, but because I was afraid. I didn't know if I wanted to risk being hurt or disappointed.

Even though the phone call was costing him plenty, he stayed on until he got a tentative "yes" from me, that I would give him a second chance and open my heart to him again.

After that I began to see a whole other side of Dave as he opened his heart and emotions to me. Pam was right. He had a tough exterior, but a soft heart inside after all. I loved getting to know that part of him.

He came in May, after nine months of being apart. I thought it would be awkward when we first met, but it wasn't at all. Our hearts were both open and engaged, and we had no end of things to talk about.

During the second semester at Multnomah, before I'd fully re-engaged my heart with Dave, I felt the Lord calling me to full-time service with Malachi Ministries in Germany. I knew there was a possibility that things wouldn't work out with Dave, but my heart was still drawn to the American teenage girls there, and I had a desire to plant myself in one location and dive into discipleship and life with them.

Since Dave was the leader of the ministry, I had to talk that through with him and ask his thoughts. He was enthusiastic and said he'd begin the process of thinking and praying about a military community where I could serve.

While I hoped that something more would develop between us, I was also content with whatever time frame it took

to know whether or not our relationship would move forward. I put my application in for full-time service, was accepted and then began to pray for God's leading as to where I would go.

Malachi Ministries was growing in full-time youth workers at the time, but the summer ministry of the Malachi singing group continued as well. Two new teams had been chosen, and needed training before leaving in mid-June. Dave asked if I would come to the training in Colorado, and then stay on for new missionary orientation and a staff conference at Horn Creek Ranch, now that I'd been accepted as a two-year missionary.

After my graduation from Multnomah, I once again left for Denver and joined him in training the new teams.

With my background in music, helping him with arrangements and vocal practices came easy. We worked well together and made a great team as we prepared the next Malachi group for their summer in Europe.

Several weeks later, after new missionary training, I flew back to Portland to wrap up things there and prepare to move to Germany at the beginning of September 1986.

God's Promise
My Spirit will lead you into all truth and show you what
is to come.
John 16:12-13

CHAPTER EIGHT

"Trust Me"

The plan was to place me in one specific military community where I'd be working with chapel youth, but over the summer a need arose for a soprano to fill a spot on the fall Malachi singing team. Dave deferred my placement into a community, and I spent September through early December leading discipleship groups, giving concerts, teaching seminars and being at weekend retreats with three others in the group.

While I enjoyed the ministry, the best part of the fall was Monday nights, our one common day off each week. In the town of St. Leon, we spent our date nights at a little Italian restaurant named Bella Capri. We sat for hours talking, sharing our hearts, telling stories about what God was doing in our ministries and falling more deeply in love.

By mid-December I'd finished my commitment to the singing team, but hadn't been placed in a military community. Although the fall had been a wonderful time of developing our relationship, we never talked about marriage, so I didn't know

where we stood. At times that was difficult, and the future seemed so uncertain for me.

Dave's often-spoken words of "Trust me" rang in my head as the days and weeks followed, and I pressed hard into seeking shelter in the Lord as I waited for both Dave's and the Lord's plans.

In mid-January we returned to Beatenberg for the annual missionary conference. Dave seemed preoccupied and busy the first few days, and we spent only short times together. In one conversation, I actually tried to put our relationship on pause after having endured probing questions from people at the conference who wanted to know what was going on between us. Since I didn't know, the only thing I could do was try to create space.

"Trust me," Dave said again.

One evening during the conference, Dave invited me to dinner. "Let's enjoy an evening together without anyone else around," he said.

We drove across the valley, through Interlaken, over to Lauterbrunnen, the small village where we'd camped the first summer with Malachi.

We took the cog train up to Murren, a village perched on the side of the mountain, with the Schilthorn towering above. In this quiet, snowy village, a horse-drawn sleigh stood waiting as we walked out of the train station. Dave motioned for me to wait while he approached the driver and asked if we could have a ride around town.

The driver said yes, and we climbed into the sleigh, wrapping warm blankets around us as the horse softly whinnied. We

took off and enjoyed a slow trot through town, the bells on the horse's harness gently ringing in the cold night air.

Magical. Breathtaking. Serene. Peaceful. Just the break I needed from the pressure within my heart.

We pulled up in front of the elegant Hotel Alpenruh and Dave asked, "Would this be a good place to have dinner?"

It looked enchanting, the perfect place to spend a peaceful evening together, I thought.

When we walked in, the server showed us to our table, which surprised me since the restaurant appeared to be full. But when we arrived at our table, I had an even bigger surprise. "Patty" was written on a pretty placard on the table.

With a little grin, Dave explained that he'd called ahead and made a reservation. And he admitted to arranging the horse-drawn sleigh as well. I was thoroughly touched by his gestures of thoughtfulness.

After a wonderful Swiss meal, the server brought the menu for dessert.

"Oh, no, I won't be having any tonight, thank you," I said as I handed the card back to her.

Dave took it out of the bewildered server's hands and put it back in mine, saying, "Well, why don't you look inside to see if perhaps there is anything you'd like for dessert," as his eyes twinkled.

In that moment I realized what was about to happen.

Dave opened the menu for me, and inside were sheaths of delicate blue paper with the words, "To My Sweetheart–January 21, 1987" written on the front cover.

My breath caught and I sat speechless. I remember looking at him wide-eyed as he asked, "Can I read it to you?"

I handed it over to him with trembling hands and then listened as he read the poem he'd written, weaving our story into lines of beautiful poetry that finished with the words, "Will you marry me?"

Just seconds later, the server, who'd been waiting off to the side, brought a silver domed tray and opened it to display a spray of roses and a sparkling diamond ring perfectly centered among them.

I don't know how long I sat there with my mouth open, with tears in my eyes, but nothing to say. I was completely and utterly surprised. Dave had to ask me the question a couple times before I finally answered a breathless, but happy "Yes!"

The restaurant full of people erupted in applause as the waitress brought beautifully prepared desserts to set on the table as she congratulated us. With the ring now on my finger, we talked for hours about all the things that we'd previously *not* talked about. "When do you want to get married? What kind of wedding do you want? How many kids do you want to have? What do you want to do with the rest of our lives?" we happily asked each other.

After deciding that we wanted to get married in March so that we could go on our Malachi youth group spring-break trip to Spain as a married couple, a funny moment occurred when he asked me how hard it would be to find a wedding dress in that short time.

"Well ... I have a little confession to make," I said, biting my lip as I spoke. "You remember when I lived in Spain? One day I was walking in Cadiz and I saw a dress in a window. It was ... well ...

everything I always wanted in a dress. And it was a really good price! I talked it all over with Jeannette and she said if I were willing to wear it for anyone, and not just for you, that it'd be okay if I bought it, even though I wasn't engaged. But I always *hoped* that I'd get to wear it for you! Do you mind that I already have my dress?"

He laughed and said, "You were really thinking about marrying me all the way back then?"

"Yes ... I've loved you for a long time, and I'm a very patient woman!"

We'd been dating for two years, and it was well worth the wait, even for this special engagement story that he'd been planning since November. He said that when I tried to put our relationship on pause a few days earlier, he nearly asked me to marry him that day, worried that I wouldn't make it a few more days. But he withstood the pressure because he wanted to give me a fairy-tale engagement, with a story to tell for years to come.

How grateful I am for that story!

We planned a wedding over the next two months, despite me going to full-time German language school and Dave coming down with a case of hepatitis. We even wrote five songs for our wedding during that time.

Back in the States, my mom worked hard to help plan the wedding. Finding dresses for my bridesmaids through a JC Penney catalog at the military PX, she then bought them, along with shoes and jewelry, without the women ever trying anything on. A friend volunteered to plan and prepare the reception, and she brought a suitcase full of things to make that happen. She, my mom, dad, brother and cousin arrived with loads of supplies, everything to make our wedding a dream come true.

On March 28, 1987, in the Gedächtniskirche, a beautiful Protestant cathedral in Speyer, Germany, we were married, with family and friends there to celebrate with us.

As the bells of the church tolled at noon, and we stepped outside on the church steps, husband and wife, I felt immense gratefulness to the Lord for his leading. Following him and his plan had brought about one of the greatest moments of my life—marrying Dave.

On the drive home from our honeymoon in Austria, we had a providential conversation that etched values into our marriage, values that have lasted over twenty-nine years thus far. As we sped down the autobahn, Dave said, "I think we should write some additional vows to the ones we said last week. We could call them the 'Ten Amendments to Our Marriage Vows.' What do you think?"

With the premise being "things we want to be true all of our married life," we began to think toward the future and what was most important as we began life as a couple.

"How about this," Dave suggested. "We want to be a cross-road, not just a signpost. When people encounter our lives, they encounter Christ in us and are faced with a choice. We don't want to just be signposts that suggest a direction, but rather compel people to make a choice."

I wrote it down as number one. And nine others like it.

2. We won't let the sun go down on our anger, but deal with conflicts the same day, at least discussing them enough that we can go to bed, committed to a peaceful resolution.

3. We will not incur debt for anything except that which will gain in value, such as a home.

4. We want the boundaries of our family to expand so that people are welcomed in and made to feel at home.

5. We will be the president of each other's fan club and never talk poorly of the other person in public. We will deal with our problems in private.

6. Anything worth doing is worth doing wrong. We want to encourage the taking of risks and failure, realizing that mistakes are necessary on the way to growth.

7. We want to raise children who have firsthand faith, faith that is their own choice, resilient in times of trouble and hardship.

8. We will strive to live life as a whole, not fragmented, recognizing that our work and family are a part of one calling to follow God and make him known.

9. We will view life as an adventure, and make sure we laugh and enjoy the journey.

10. We will continually reach for the depths of intimacy in marriage, knowing that it's a preview of our union with Christ.

After writing all those down in Dave's thick, black notebook, we hurried home to St. Leon, content with each other, and the sweetness of our earliest days of marriage fresh in our memories.

God's Promise
I have prepared amazing things for those who love me.
1 Corinthians 2:9

CHAPTER NINE

Under Investigation

A s we settled into life as a married couple, Dave continued leading the work of Malachi Ministries, as well as being the youth leader on the military base in Karlsruhe. With a community of just over two hundred teenagers, seventy regularly came to our youth group each week, which made a significant impact in their lives, the youth group and their high school.

We chaperoned dances at the school, and attended sports games and musical programs. We ran youth group on Wednesday nights, and were in Karlsruhe on Sundays for church. We spent Sunday afternoons having lunch with friends who hosted us each week, and then held a ministry team meeting with our core kids who wanted to reach their high school for Christ. We loved those kids, and gave our hearts to them and the community, as well as the chapel family.

Chaplain Bill*, our head chaplain on base, was supportive of our work with young people. He loved helping us reach

* Names changed for privacy

students with the gospel and often would drive the Army bus to retreats. He was one of our greatest allies in the ministry.

But in military communities people are transferred every few years, and others come to replace them. Within a year of our being there as a married couple, Bill got his orders to move on. We grieved his leaving, as he was not only helpful to the youth group, but a friend as well. Also, his daughter had been an integral part of our youth group, and we would miss her vivaciousness and love for Christ, which drew kids in.

Bill left at the beginning of the summer, and there was a lull in leadership at the chapel until the next chaplain came in as his replacement. We continued on throughout the summer, and saw kids come to Christ at different events and Bible studies we had during those months.

In September 1988 the new chaplain arrived, and we went to see him shortly afterward. We wanted to introduce ourselves, let him know what we were doing and ask how we could help to support him as he came into his new chapel community.

We were met with little warmth. His replies to our questions were curt, and he was not quick to make eye contact during our conversation. We left confused and unsure of what the road ahead would be like with this man as our chaplain.

But at youth group that evening, in our cozy attic meeting space with a room full of lively teenagers interested in spiritual things, we forgot about the cold reception from Chaplain Matt*. We focused on the kids and had a great time, as usual.

* Names changed for privacy

The chaplain was again distant during the service at chapel the next week, and we began to wonder if there was something going on that we weren't aware of. There was no reason to think it had anything to do with us, so we assumed it had to do with chapel business, and that we would carry on as usual despite the cold front.

But on Wednesday when we arrived for youth group, we found the door to our attic meeting space locked. Our key wouldn't open the door.

My heart pounded as we walked to the chapel to find out if someone had a new key for us.

We got more than that.

"Dave, Connie, come into my office and close the door," Chaplain Matt tersely ordered. "Today is your last youth group. You're to turn in your keys now. Your contract is not being re-newed. I wish you the best."

Dave opened his mouth to ask a question, but was met with a hard stare and the words, "That will be all." We'd been fired, and we didn't know why.

I began to cry as we walked out. My mind was racing. *How can this be happening? How can he do this to us? What will the kids say? Will the parents rally around us? What about the com-mander of the Army post? Does he know Chaplain Matt is doing this to us? Why is God letting this happen?*

Dave was calm, put his hand around my shoulder and pulled me in tight. "I don't know what's going on, but God does, and he's going to see us through this. We'll get answers. This isn't the end yet."

But it was.

With great turmoil in our hearts, we told the kids good-bye on the steps of the chapel that night, not even able to have one last youth group meeting. We tried not to be accusatory toward Chaplain Matt, but it was hard to explain what was going on.

Dave was quick to turn them to the Lord and say, "Bad things happen to good people, but God can redeem those things. We don't know what his purposes are right now, but we know he's good and we know he loves each of us. So we're going to pray, seek answers and trust him for what's ahead."

We stood in a huge circle and prayed together, the tears flowing as we finished and said our goodbyes.

The ride home to St. Leon that night was silent. I was hurt, angry, confused and deeply saddened by what had just taken place. Dave was contemplative, prayerful and levelheaded, determined to get to the bottom of it.

Within two days, we received a phone call that would begin that process.

"David Craig Patty? This is CID, the investigative division of the American military. You're being put under investigation for financial fraud and mishandling of government funds. You'll be receiving a call shortly with instructions for taking your deposition, both you and your wife. Each will be taken privately and you're not to discuss it with each other. Your contract has been suspended until further notice, and you are not to set foot on the Karlsruhe post unless you are there for official CID business. Do you understand me?"

Life as we had known it had just ceased.

I wrestled desperately with God in the weeks to come. Following him was not easy when I couldn't make sense of what he was doing.

A flurry of phone calls went back and forth, from students and parents and members of the chapel community.

"We love you. We're in full support of you."

"How could they take away the best thing this community has ever had?"

"It'll all work out, and you'll be back before you know it."

"Is there anything we can do to help you?"

Everyone's kind words and sentiments were no balm for the ache in my heart. I missed our kids. I didn't understand. And I was mad at God for allowing this.

There were days when I sat in our living room, from morning until dark, trying to make sense of it all. Dave tried to coax me out to do things, or at least to cook a meal. But I was despondent. I cried for hours, and couldn't open my Bible or pray.

After two weeks of no news, we received a phone call from CID requesting us to be on post to give our depositions the following Monday morning. As we drove to Karlsruhe a few days later, I felt as though I'd already been put in prison, and I didn't even know for what.

They took Dave and me to separate rooms, and for hours we were questioned. I felt faint when we were finally released. I just wanted to go home and crawl in bed to hide from the world.

Their questions made no sense to me. They wanted to know details about our retreats, about how we financed them, about who was involved, what my husband's role was in the chapel, and in what capacities I had been involved.

There were questions about Chaplain Bill, about the chapel assistants, about the choir director and the children's workers. They even wanted to know what kinds of conversations and contacts I'd had with the secretary and the chaplain's wife.

Again, I cried for days. Dave finally persuaded me to at least sit with him on the couch and let him read the Bible to me. But it didn't penetrate, as my heart was hard. I accused God of abandoning us. And I told him I didn't know if I could trust him or follow him anymore. This was the most devastating thing that had ever happened to me. It felt cruel and unfair.

In the meantime, Dave was getting phone calls from chaplains on other bases where we had Malachi staff.

"I just got a call from CID about you. What's going on?"

"Hey, I just want you to know that I still believe in what Malachi's doing and until they tell me otherwise, I'll keep my Malachi worker on my staff."

"I'm getting wind of some pretty rough times for your ministry's presence on military bases. You're valuable to us, I hope you make it."

"Is there anything I can do for you?"

Several weeks later Dave got another phone call from the USAREUR (US Army Europe) office in Heidelberg. "This is Sergeant Clark* calling on behalf of Chaplain Hayes* from the chief of chaplain's office at USAREUR," the sergeant explained. "He would like to meet with you at your earliest convenience. Would it be possible for you to come to headquarters day after tomorrow?"

Not knowing if this was in connection with the investigation, Dave put on his suit jacket and headed into the chaplain's office two days later.

Chaplain Hayes served as the deputy to the chief of chaplains, whom Dave had met on several prior occasions, under better circumstances.

"I called you in today to let you know that there have been some regulation changes in Army policy on ID cards concerning contractors. They're clamping down on the number of IDs that can be issued to contractors, and I'm sorry to tell you that all ID cards of your Malachi staff will be revoked at the end of the month."

When the Army makes regulation changes, there's no chance for rebuttal. It was a done deal, and there was nothing more to say. We met for our regular staff meeting the next Friday, and Dave gave the news.

"How will we get on base to meet with students?" our staff asked.

"Will I still be able to meet kids at the bowling alley or the snack bar?" others asked.

"What happens when there's a crisis and they close the base to all but ID cardholders? What will I do about getting to chapel and youth group?"

"Will this affect my ability to work in and among the Army system?"

These were legitimate questions, and ones Dave didn't have answers for yet.

The lid was clamping down on us hard in those dark November days. In my despondent state, I wondered if this

spelled the end of our ministry there. Between the loss of ID card privileges, the ongoing investigation and the fact that it seemed in the military system you were guilty until proven innocent, we were in a bad spot.

Several weeks later, at another Malachi meeting in our home, Dave spoke strongly to our staff. "These may seem like dark days, but they should not come as a surprise to us. We know that there will be suffering and persecution for the sake of the gospel, so we should count it as a privilege to be in that spot right now."

It didn't seem like a privilege to me. It was hard to see my way through the suffering and see it as persecution. Maybe we'd done something wrong and were being rightfully punished for it, even though I didn't know what it could possibly have been.

But Dave continued, "I want to read to you from 1 Peter 4:19: 'So then, those who suffer accordingly to God's will should commit themselves to their faithful Creator and continue to do good.'

"That's what I want us to do. Even though this is a tough place for all of us, I want us to press in to the Lord, trust his will, and continue to do good. Can you do that? And we're not leaving, even if our ID cards are revoked and we never get them back again. If God wants us to stay here and minister to his kids, he will make a way for us to do that. We're not backing off, we're not going home and we're not giving up!"

His words resonated in my head over the coming weeks, and I felt myself beginning a slow path back to the Lord.

I really did want to follow him, to say yes and accept what had happened. That had been my heart for years before. I was

actually discouraged with myself that I was so easily blown off course at the first sign of real trouble. It didn't look like I was doing much trusting of the Lord or following his ways. With his help, I wanted to change that.

We shopped off base at German stores, and figured out other ways to meet with students, in places that didn't require an ID card. It took creativity, but our staff was able to find ways to share their lives and the gospel, despite the setback of no ID cards.

Dave heard bits and pieces about the ongoing investigation over the coming months. He knew that they'd sent military investigators to the States to deposition some of our volunteers who'd left because of normal military transfers. And by now we knew that Chaplain Bill was under investigation as well.

I spent those long winter months reading Psalms, comforted by the times that David, and other psalmists, had been persecuted and suffered. They even asked God "why," though they often returned their hearts to him with praise, no matter what.

I sought to do the same.

God's Promise
I will be your safe place in difficult times.
Nahum 1:7

CHAPTER TEN

Trauma at Sea

We went ahead with plans for another spring break trip to Spain. We still had the support of chaplains in the communities where the rest of our staff worked, and so pressed ahead with hopes that there would be a breakthrough soon. We prayed that this event would be a breath of fresh air as we spent time with the teenagers we loved so much.

Some of our Karlsruhe kids signed up to go, even though no youth group had continued after we left. They came under our wing for the week, and it felt good to have at least a few of "our kids" join us on the trip.

All twelve buses met up at a *parkplatz* along the German autobahn, so that six hundred students and staff could caravan together through France, and on to the coast of Spain to Barcelona, where we'd catch a ferry over to the island of Mallorca.

But at some point during the night, our bus was separated from the other eleven. The bus driver admitted that he'd gotten lost, and that it'd taken him a while to get turned around and back on the right road. Thus we didn't make it to the dock in time to catch the first ferry.

These were the days before cell phones, so we weren't in contact with anyone on those eleven buses. I remember Dave putting his head in his hands and praying as we rolled along through the Spanish countryside. I knew he was feeling the weight of responsibility for all six hundred staff and students, and that he couldn't be there to oversee the loading of the ferry. Nor would we make the crossing with them.

We learned later that other Malachi men took charge of loading students and staff onto the ship, trying to get the captain to wait for our bus. However, the captain and crew were concerned because of the weather. They knew a storm was brewing and wanted to get the ferry on its way. The decision was made to set sail immediately.

Many male Malachi staff members decided to stay behind to wait for our arrival, so the ferry set off with 560 passengers, including all our female Malachi staff, volunteers from different communities, chaplains and the teenagers.

In the meantime, our bus arrived at the dock an hour after that ferry had sailed. The Malachi men who had stayed behind had worked with the ferry agency to secure passage on another smaller ferry, which was scheduled to leave at 10 p.m. We arrived around 9 p.m., so barely had time to unload everything off the bus and onto the ferry before departure.

The crew was agitated. "*Rápido, rápido,*" they shouted.

While Dave and the men dealt with the luggage, I got the students who'd been on our bus aboard. The wind howled, rain battered the windows and the small ferry was already rocking from side to side though we hadn't even left the harbor. There was definitely fear in the air as we waited for everyone to come aboard.

Finally, with everyone seated, the ferry launched. Just minutes after passing out of the harbor, it lurched violently, sending students and adults to the floor. One of our students, Angie, made her way into my arms and we clung to each other. Within an hour, people were losing their dinners. Crew members came around to pass out little white bags. With one violent lurch after another, those white bags were in great demand. Both Angie and I needed them constantly for the next hours.

The passage was agonizingly slow. The bags began to tip over, and the only noise in the cabin was the retching of stomachs. The groans were horrendous as people began to dry heave.

It was supposed to be a four-hour trip. After three hours, Dave went to the crew. Speaking Spanish, he asked, "It's been three hours, and we have just one more to go, right?"

They laughed in his face.

He returned to his seat, his head in his hands.

Suddenly, we heard a wave crash over the boat, it tipped farther to the right than it ever had and people and things were violently tossed to the side and onto the floor. At that point, the crying started, with men and women alike sobbing in fear. Dave didn't cry, but only because he was trying to hold it together as the leader.

I was sobbing, along with Angie. We clutched hands and prayed aloud, asking Jesus to rescue us. In those moments I thought, *If this is what hell is like, I'm glad I'll never know.* I couldn't imagine how much more horrendous it could be.

Four hours passed, five hours, six hours. And still no end in sight.

Silence overtook the cabin, with only a few whimpers now and then. I tried to close my eyes and rest for a few minutes, but just when I started to doze, another violent lurch seized us and the terror started again.

One of the comforts that kept me going was that at least the other larger ferry had made it out in time, and was probably already there by now. So if our ferry went down, at least the other 560 would be spared. I truly believed we wouldn't make it.

I couldn't imagine what it would be like for those of our staff who were separated from their spouses or Malachi partners. It would be agonizing for them to go on if we all were to die. As the sun came up, and there was no sign of land, it appeared hopeless.

The crew was no help. By this time many were drunk, likely out of fear, and who knew the condition of the captain? It certainly felt like there was a drunken sailor at the helm. I truly thought we would never see land again, and began to prepare myself for meeting Jesus.

After twelve agonizing hours on the boat from hell, someone finally spotted land.

I was in the fetal position, still holding Angie, waiting for the final wave to crash over us and send us to a watery grave,

when the feeble voice called out, "I think I see land," and a few crawled to the windows.

Sure enough, they could see it. It took another two hours to reach the shore, but we did.

I have never been happier to walk on land than I was that day. Unsure of what had happened to the other ferry, Dave asked someone on the dock if they knew anything.

It was good news.

Although a wave had shattered a window, although they, too, had endured twelve hours of agony, they were safe at the hotel. Later, those on the first ferry told us what thought had comforted them during the crossing: "If we go down, at least the other ferry surely must've seen the storm and didn't go out into it. God will have spared them."

Thanks to the Lord's saving protection, we all survived and headed into a week that would turn out to be one of the most exciting retreats of our lives.

Students were open spiritually, probably because of the terror and trauma they'd just survived. Within days, kids were putting their faith in Christ and rising resiliently above what had happened.

The sun eventually came out, and we carried on with fun and games as if we'd never lived through the terror. But kids' lives were changed, as were ours. Like us, people are probably still telling the story to this day, as well as wearing the T-shirts one of the chaplains had made in town: "I survived the Choke and Barf Ferry." He sold out of those T-shirts before the end of the week.

After that traumatic event, I returned home to Germany with a renewed sense of trust in God and a desire to follow

him, even though our difficult circumstances had not been resolved.

Within a few days of our arrival back home, Dave got another phone call from the USAREUR chaplain's office asking him to come in.

The DCINC (Deputy Commander in Chief) of the chief of chaplain's office welcomed him into his office. After pleasantries, the chaplain got down to business. "Dave, I'm wondering if you could share with me about Malachi Ministries. Start from the beginning and give me a rundown on how you came about, what your mission is and where things are currently at."

Not knowing why he was being asked, or if it had anything to do with the investigation, Dave gave the history and background of Malachi, and shared the heart and vision he had for the ministry.

When Dave finished, the chaplain leaned back in his chair, folded his hands in front of him and said, "I've been tasked by the chief of chaplains to gather as much information about you as possible, in order for us to follow through on a command from the two-star general at USAREUR, who wants to find a way to restore your ID cards."

Wow. That came as a shock. Our hands had been tied, and there had been no one to turn to except the Lord. Now a general was tasking this office with finding a way to untie our hands.

As the weeks went by, Dave learned more about what was behind this request. The general had kids in a youth program in one of the military chapels. He got wind of the ID cards being revoked and started asking questions.

To this day we don't know if he was a believer, but God used him in a significant way to light a fire under the chaplain's office. The chief chaplain at the time was not especially supportive of our ministry, but when one's commanding officer gives a direct order, it's one's obligation to follow through.

So for the next two months, the restoration of our ID cards was the deputy's priority. He investigated what it would take to get us our ID cards back, and discovered that it was virtually impossible. He reported this to the general: "There is only one solution, but that solution requires amending the SOFA."

The original SOFA (Status of Forces Agreement) that was signed between the US and Germany in 1951, allowing an American military presence in that country, would have to be amended in order for ID cards to be issued to Malachi staff. A document between the US and German ambassador would have to be signed saying that Malachi Ministries was an essential support to the presence of the American military. This would grant the same status to Malachi as was granted to organizations such as the Red Cross and Boy Scouts.

At the conclusion of his report, the chaplain made it clear to the general that he didn't think we were essential.

The general disagreed.

We later heard that when he heard the chaplain's report he had just three words for him: "Make it happen."

In June of 1989, in Bonn at the seat of Germany's government, the amendment was ratified. Malachi was written into the SOFA, allowing all Malachi workers who were on contract with the US military in Germany to be granted full ID privileges.

The ID cards we'd had revoked were limited. We were only able to use them for shopping at the Shoppette (a 7-Eleven type store) and getting on base for necessary activities. We couldn't shop at the PX or commissary, nor did we have APO privileges (being able to mail through the US Postal system). Our limited IDs were taken away, but God replaced them with something even better: full ID cards.

The amendment was to take effect immediately.

The following summer, Desert Storm launched. The bases went on full lockdown and allowed in only those with *full* ID cardprivileges. God saw that coming, and made a way to keep us on base and in contact with students during such a trying time.

It was an amazing day when Dave and I walked out of the Army office that issued ID cards, holding our own in our hands. The miracle that this represented was beyond our wildest imaginations. We were grateful to the Lord for his power that had used an Army general to accomplish his will.

Shortly afterward, Dave made a call to the judiciary office in Kaiserslautern, asking for a meeting with the man in command. We'd heard rumors that the investigation was complete, but no one had contacted us to say what the findings were, though we assumed the charges against Dave had been dropped since no one had shown up at our door to handcuff him!

The commanding officer was a believer, and knew of Malachi. He was able to fill in the gaps on what had taken place, and why Dave had been put under investigation.

There were never any charges levied against us that had validity. Instead, it was someone else who was being investigated, and we were the pawns they were using against the other person.

When Dave asked if all charges had been dropped, the commanding officer said, "Yes, they were dropped several months ago."

"Why wasn't I contacted? I still have chaplains in communities asking me about the investigation because they were called and questioned about their involvement with Malachi. They want to know if we were cleared. Could you send something out across the chaplaincy in Germany to verify that my name has been exonerated?"

"Unfortunately, we're unable to do that," he replied. "It's against policy."

We had to go back to Exodus 14:14, a verse that we'd claimed over and over ... during those dark days, asking God to fight our battle: "The Lord will fight for you; you need only to be still."

While it had been tempting to fight the battle on our own, we knew there was no way we'd be able to defend ourselves. It left us with just one choice: to let the Lord fight for us.

And he had, in a much more powerful way than we ever could have. Although no official clearing of Dave's name or Malachi Ministries ever took place, word made it around the Army chapels that the charges had been cleared. God got his work done, despite the persecution.

Plus, the roots of my faith that had been so severely tested over the prior months had grown deeper and wider. This provided me with a much purer and richer faith than I'd ever had before.

It would hold me firm through what was to come the following year.

God's Promise
The Lord will fight for you; you need only to be still.
Exodus 14:14

CHAPTER ELEVEN

Winds of Change

In the summer of 1989 Dave had the privilege of attending the Lausanne Congress in Manila, Philippines. While our ministry had been to American military dependent teenagers, Dave's heart still beat for seeing the gospel taken throughout the world, and he was thrilled to join more than four thousand participants as they discussed evangelism for nine days.

It was also an opportunity for him to visit the place of his birth, Subic Bay, Philippines, where his parents had been missionaries with OCSC when he was born.

His family had come back to the States on furlough when he was just four years old, and then stayed when his dad was asked to become the executive director for OCSC in 1966. They lived in Denver throughout his youth, while his dad served at the home office until 1979. At that time they moved to Germany, and his dad became the European director.

Having sensed God's call to missions when he was twelve years old while on a trip around the world with his dad, Dave expected to one day serve as a missionary in a cross-cultural setting. Where that would be, and when, he didn't know. But he expected it to happen at some point.

Dave had let me know that fact the day after we were engaged, while on a ski lift in Switzerland. High in the Alps, sunshine on our faces, looking out over the snow-covered mountains, he turned to me and said, "I just want to make sure you know that someday we may move far away and become missionaries in another culture. Are you willing for that?"

Young and in love, I happily replied that I'd go anywhere in the world with him. And I meant it. Or at least, I thought I did.

While Dave was in the Philippines, I went with a group of teenagers and some of our Malachi staff to the (at that time) Communist country of Yugoslavia. On the island of Ugljan, off the coast of Zadar, we met up with a group of Yugoslav families for a week of camp in a secluded area owned and quietly operated by Christians.

I met a Yugoslavian woman who shared her story of conversion with me, and I was captivated by the courage she had in choosing to follow Christ in a place where Christians were marginalized at best, and persecuted at worst.

I couldn't imagine what it was like to live in a country this beautiful, and not be free to proclaim my faith to others. My heart was moved to even more deeply follow the Lord myself, and I came away from that week with gratefulness for the freedom I had to do that.

The winds of change were blowing across Eastern Europe the following summer, as protests began to emerge in Poland, Bulgaria, East Germany and Czechoslovakia. By mid-fall, the news was dominated by reports of people spontaneously gathering in the streets of cities to protest the oppressive governments of those countries.

Dave and I were in the States for a few weeks in November and watched in awe, glued to the TV, as the Berlin Wall was torn down, and thousands of East Germans flooded into West Germany. After so many years of living there, and particularly having worked among American military personnel who were protecting the very borders that had just been broken through, we were sad to be in the US during this momentous occasion, as the Cold War began its end. We returned to Germany a few weeks later, listening to firsthand reports of what the fall of the Berlin Wall had been like.

By the end of the year, the governments had toppled in Poland, Czechoslovakia, East Germany, Bulgaria, Hungary and Romania. As we drove on the autobahn that December, we were amazed to see little Trabants, the East German-made cars, on the roads, carrying wide-eyed people who were seeing life in the Western world, many for the first time.

Fresh from having been at the Lausanne Congress, Dave was ecstatic at the thought of being able to now bring the gospel into those countries, particularly to freely share it with young people. He began to envision something that could be done that very summer to reach out to teenagers in former Communist countries.

Other significant events were taking place at the same time: in January 1990 we learned that we were expecting our first child. After two and half years of marriage, we were delighted and excited at the prospect of being parents. Fully reveling in this good news, we were thankful for God's gift to us, and it wasn't long before we were talking about names and making plans not only to prepare for his or her arrival, but for what our future family would be like.

Plans were also in full swing for another Malachi spring break trip, this time to the island of Ibiza, also off the coast of Spain.

Although the year before had been a difficult, traumatic trip, it had fueled many students' faith and they were excited to invite their friends to experience something similar, though we hoped it wouldn't include a long, traumatic ferry ride! We expected another large turnout.

The door had never opened for us to return to ministry in Karlsruhe after the investigation had finished, but God opened a new door into Heidelberg at Patrick Henry Village chapel, known as PHV. Under the leadership of an excellent chaplain, we began working with the youth group there that fall. Many of our students were excited about going with us on the spring break trip to Ibiza, and we looked forward to seeing what God would do in their lives.

Then the unexpected happened.

Just four months pregnant, I began to experience some difficulties toward the end of February. With our spring break trip weeks away, I anxiously hoped for the doctor's okay that all was well with the baby, and that I could make the trip with our youth group. I adored the girls I'd been having Bible study with over the past months, and I was looking forward to a whole week with them in Spain.

Then my German doctor, Dr. Stork (yes, that was really her name) delivered the news: "You must go to bed immediately. You're in danger of losing the baby."

That day, she put me on bed rest, indefinitely.

Shocked, I returned home to climb in bed and make sense of this news. The thought that something could be wrong with our baby, or worse, that we'd lose him or her, had never occurred to me. Prior to this, pregnancy had seemed like any other life event. In my naïveté, I thought I would get pregnant, spend nine months of normal life just getting a little bigger as the baby grew, give birth, go home and carry on with normal life.

Now I was faced with the possibility of a much different scenario.

Dave left a few weeks later to lead the spring break trip, while I stayed home. I grieved not being able to go with Dave and our students, but also knew there was no choice but to follow my doctor's orders. I didn't want to do anything that would put our baby in jeopardy.

I am thankful that my mom offered to fly from the States and stay with me that week, since I wasn't allowed out of bed. She spent the week not only cooking and caring for me, but sewing for the baby's room, while I faithfully read *What to Expect When You're Expecting*, trying to learn as much as possible about what was ahead. I continued to pray that the Lord would protect this little one and see him or her to the due date in late August.

After Dave and the team returned from a fruitful spring break retreat, plans began to take shape for Malachi's first missions trip into one of the former Eastern bloc countries, Hungary.

Dave had been in contact with missionaries who had connections in Budapest. He made arrangements to bring our American military kids into a Hungarian English-speaking high school for a week. The students could practice English during the day and show the American students their city and lives. In the evenings, our staff and students could tell them about Jesus.

Excitement ran high as students and staff alike envisioned entering a country where the gospel had been off-limits just months before.

Still on bed rest three months later, I knew I wouldn't be joining them. Although I was sad to miss this historic event, I knew my job would be to pray throughout the two-week trip as they traveled into the country for a time of training, and then on to Budapest for a week with the Hungarian students. Dave, our Malachi staff and the fifty American students going with them made final preparations for leaving at the end of June.

Then the unexpected happened, again.

Up late one night while Dave worked on materials he'd teach at Lake Balaton for training our students how to share their faith, I began to feel uneasy. Something didn't feel right inside me, though it was hard to tell if it was just the growing baby shifting, or if there was actually something wrong. I read through *What to Expect* looking for clues about what was going on.

By morning, it was clear that at thirty-two weeks of pregnancy, I was having signs of labor. Dave drove me to the hospital in Schwetzingen, where we'd planned to deliver under Dr. Stork's guidance. Within a half hour of arrival, I was admitted. Monitors were strapped on and IV inserted.

Any German language I'd had stored away in my head was forgotten, and I became completely dependent on Dave for all translation about what was happening. "Your wife is in labor," the doctor said to Dave in German. "It's too soon for the baby to come so we're going to try and stop it, if we can."

The next two days were tense. Dave stayed by my side as much as possible, all the while communicating with our team, who were just days away from the trip to Hungary, wondering if Dave would be going or not.

Labor finally slowed, but I was on a steady drip of tocolytic drugs to keep labor at bay as they carefully monitored the baby and me.

With the trip to Hungary now imminent, it was agonizing as we talked through our options. Dave consulted with the doctors, gathering as much information as possible about what they anticipated, and whether or not they thought I was out of the danger zone for delivering the baby prematurely. The night before the group was to leave for Hungary, he asked the doctor, "What is your prognosis?"

"We're going to do everything we can to keep this baby inside your wife right now. The baby is small and it's too early for its arrival. We'll keep your wife in the hospital indefinitely until we're sure the situation is stable."

Then the question we really needed to ask: "Do you think this baby will be born within the next two weeks?"

The doctor shrugged, "There is no way of telling that. We plan to do everything we can to make sure it's not born before then, but you can never say for sure."

Back in my room, with the light of day fading, and an early morning departure ahead, Dave and I had a long, tearful conversation.

"I won't go to Hungary. I'll put someone else in charge and stay here with you," Dave said to me as he held my hand on the edge of the hospital bed. "There is no way I'm going to miss the birth of our first child, or let you go through this alone. I won't leave you."

While he'd been speaking with the doctor, and in fact, for the three days I'd been in the hospital, I'd been crying out to the Lord about what was going on. After initial shock, then grief, then anger, I'd somehow, only by God's grace, come to a peaceful place in my heart by that evening.

"I think you should go," I said quietly. "I've been praying about it ever since I was admitted. I had a feeling it was going to come down to this moment. I think the Lord wants me to trust him and release you to go."

I didn't say these words easily. Though there was peace in my heart, I also knew that there was a pretty good chance it meant Dave wouldn't be there for the birth. That thought brought instant tears to my eyes, but still I knew that God was asking this of me.

"What's the worst thing that could happen? I deliver and you're not here. We'd survive that. It seems like this trip is really

important. I don't know why, but I think we'd both regret it if you didn't go."

Dave laid his head down beside me on the bed, and we both cried.

Watching him walk out of my dark room that night, I wept until I had no more tears. Everything in me wanted to call out to him to come back and stay with me. But I knew that this step of obedience, this act of following what I believed the Lord was asking of me, was the only thing I could do. I had no assurance that the baby wouldn't be born before he returned. But I did have an assurance of the Lord's presence with me, no matter what happened.

It was just me, baby and the Lord in that hospital room.

God's Promise
I will cover you with my feathers and protect you with my wings.
Psalm 91:4

CHAPTER TWELVE

A Seed Is Planted

Although it would be two weeks until I heard the news, the trip to Hungary was truly a significant mark in the history of Malachi Ministries, and in our lives as well.

After the training at Lake Balaton, they arrived in Budapest and began the week of sharing their lives, and the gospel, with students and teachers alike.

The Hungarian teenagers were unbelievably receptive as they opened their homes and hearts to the Americans. Days were spent out in the city, visiting castles, walking for hours, eating homemade food from Hungarian homes, and sharing life together with little difference between the teenagers from the two vastly different countries.

The evenings were fun and intense. Laughter rang out as games were played, and everyone joined in singing songs about God. Students gave their testimonies, and "The Jesus Film" was shown.

On the last night, when given the opportunity to respond to the gospel, many Hungarian students stayed up late into the night talking with our staff and students about the things they'd seen and heard during the week. A number of teenagers put their faith in Jesus, hungry to learn more about him.

Dave spent a lot of time with the director of the school during that week. While open to the exchange of students, she was not as open to the gospel.

"It is my philosophy that our lives are like a rose bush. It grows and blooms, producing a beautiful, fragrant flower. But then it dies and goes back into the ground. I believe we all end up as food for rose bushes," Aniko explained.

"My daughter once found a book that told the story of how Jesus died. She asked me why it had to happen, and if he really did rise from the dead. I told her that it's a very nice story, and would be even nicer if it was true. But I think it is only a fairy tale, and that when our lives are over, that's it. There is nothing else."

Dave's heart broke for Aniko, and for the people of her city and country. As he looked out over Budapest from the seventeenth floor of the apartment building he was staying in, he wept and prayed over the city, asking God to make himself known there. He prayed that tens of thousands of young people would proclaim him as Lord, not only here, but across Eastern Europe.

A seed was planted that night.

Meanwhile, I stayed in the hospital, being monitored three times a day by ultrasounds and undergoing numerous tests. During one of those ultrasounds, the technician turned to me as she moved the wand over my protruding belly and said in

German, "Aha! I know what you're having! Do you want to know?"

Up until this time, Dave and I didn't want to know the sex of our baby before birth. It seemed a more romantic thought to discover it together in the delivery room after nine months of waiting. But in that moment, I needed some encouragement. After hesitating for just a moment, I blurted out, "Yes, I want to know!"

"It's a boy!" she proclaimed.

A boy! This was no longer just "baby," but a baby boy named Tyler Joseph. Our Tyler! I could hardly contain the glee bubbling inside me. We'd already chosen a boy name and a girl name, so we'd be ready no matter who arrived. I was beyond thrilled to know this news, but kept it to myself in the coming days, hoping I'd get to be the one to share it with Dave.

Finally, on July 4, I was discharged from the hospital, still pregnant. The doctors were pleased that they'd been able to halt labor, and assured me that the baby wasn't in danger. However, as a precaution, I was put back on bed rest until the end of July. By that time, I would be at the end of thirty-six weeks, and they felt the baby would be healthy enough to come any time after that.

My mother-in-law, Margaret, picked me up that day and took me to her house in St. Leon, where I would stay until Dave arrived home a few days later. It was a huge relief to be out of the hospital and at my in-laws for those days.

Our reunion was a tearful and sweet one. How we praised the Lord together for protecting the baby, Dave and me during those days. I was so grateful to be back together, now awaiting Tyler's arrival later in August.

With me still on bed rest, and no rush to prepare things for his arrival, we spent the next two weeks living quietly, spending time together and sharing all that had taken place in our lives while we'd been apart.

But on the morning of July 19, all of that changed. Labor set in intensely and we rushed off to the hospital once again. I was put back on the same ward, and they once again administered the drugs that would hold off delivery. Although I was nearing the thirty-six-week mark, they felt Tyler was too small and wanted to give him more time, particularly to develop his lungs.

By evening, contractions had stopped, and it seemed we'd averted labor once again. I even walked the halls that night, holding on to Dave's arm with one hand, and steering my IV pole with the other.

The next morning, I lay in bed reading; sure I'd be released later that day, I was thinking about what to make for dinner that night as I looked at recipes in the magazine I held. I was also thinking about the fact that we hadn't put the baby's room together yet and that we'd better get started on it soon once we arrived back home.

Dave was at the hospital by 9 a.m. Hours crept by as we waited for news of my release. But at one in the afternoon, we were still there. Nurses had been in and out, observing the monitor and quietly jotting notes on their charts. But no one said anything to us. We waited for the doctor to arrive.

At 1:30, he entered my room, looked at the monitor and rapidly said something to Dave before departing.

Unaware of what he'd said, I continued to read my *Good Housekeeping* magazine. But not for long.

"Did you understand what he said?" Dave asked with concern in his eyes.

"No, why?" I answered.

As he began to reply, a team of nurses briskly walked in with a cart and a mission.

"He said the baby's in danger and they're going to take him right now. By caesarean. We're having this baby today."

I was still processing the shock of this news as the nurses prepped me and wheeled me out of the room. Dave jogged alongside my bed while they whisked me to the operating room. A quick kiss, a tender look and assurances of prayer, and then I was taken inside, alone. A mask was put over my face, and I smelled a whiff of anesthesia. I was out in seconds.

Due to full anesthesia, I was aware of nothing for hours beyond that. I didn't know they allowed Dave to be in the room. I didn't hear Tyler's first cry. I don't remember them placing Tyler on me, though Dave says I cradled him with my one free arm.

Yet, despite all the signs showing Tyler was in danger, he was born healthy at 2:30 p.m. on July 20, 1990.

I woke hours later, feeling like a truck had run over me. Holding Tyler in his arms, Dave rushed to my side. I was only able to ask, "Is he okay?" before falling back into my anesthetized stupor.

It was a long recovery for me, and for Tyler, who ended up with a bad case of jaundice and had to be under the bilirubin lights for over a week. He and I were in the hospital for twelve days on what I have since fondly called our "German Vacation."

In the meantime, Dave worked like crazy at home, wallpapering, painting and setting up furniture for the day when we were finally released, ending a turbulent eight-month stretch of

life. But we had a healthy, albeit small, boy and were so relieved to head home and begin life as a family of three on that sunny July day at the end of the month.

I have often reflected back on that time, not with anger or bitterness, but with deep gratefulness and genuine fondness for how the Lord carried us through those months. It wasn't the pregnancy I anticipated, or the type of birth I imagined. In fact, I remember thinking as the nurses were wheeling me away for the caesarean, *I never read that part of the book!* It was probably just as well.

This was one of the first times I made a conscious decision, in the midst of a very difficult situation, to say yes immediately to God's ways and trust his promise to keep me under his wings.

The roots of my faith went much deeper after this experience. I realized that my relationship with the Lord had deepened so fully that I could've even gone through Tyler's birth without Dave and come out fine on the other side. While I missed Dave terribly those two weeks, the Lord had been so near to me in the hospital that I knew him in a different way than I had before. And I liked this new depth of relationship between us.

As I recovered from the C-section and began mothering, I felt, yet again, as if a different person was emerging. I didn't feel as fragile, and my fears were not as great as they had once been. I'd walked through a fire, and come out alive, maybe even smelling sweeter, afterward.

God's Promise
When you walk through the fires of adversity, you will
not be burned.
Isaiah 43:2

CHAPTER THIRTEEN

God's Calling

At just three months old, Tyler took his first airplane trip to the States. After being showered in love and gifts by family, friends and our church families in Washington and Colorado, we continued on to Wheaton, Illinois. Dave's brother, Steve, was studying at Wheaton College getting his master's degree at that time.

While Tyler and I spent time with dear friends who had served with us in Karlsruhe and now lived in Wheaton, Dave and Steve spent hours talking about the program he was in, with Steve recommending that Dave come study there too.

The program was full of excellent professors, with an emphasis on understanding educational theory and its application to helping people grow in their faith through the church and other Christian contexts.

It seemed like an ideal fit for Dave. As he continued to think about how to better ground the students we worked with in their faith and in the Word of God, he knew the tools he'd gain

there would be invaluable for the future of Malachi's ministry in Germany.

Several months later he applied to the program at Wheaton, and was accepted. The OCSC board granted him a year's educational furlough, and he made provisions for a temporary transfer of leadership since we intended to return to Malachi after his studies. He was awarded the Billy Graham scholarship, a full-tuition grant for furloughing missionaries, a generous provision from the Lord that made it possible for us to afford his schooling.

Dave left Germany ahead of me, needing to be at Wheaton College for orientation in late August. I wanted to be at one final staff conference, so Tyler and I stayed a few more weeks, and then traveled to Chicago where we were happily reunited with Dave.

Because the missionary furlough home that we were to live in was not yet completed, we moved into our friends' home for three weeks and began to get oriented to life in the States, as well as to Dave's school schedule.

Not wanting to be gone from Malachi for too long, he stacked classes upon classes so that he would finish the degree in one year, instead of the recommended two. The goal was to graduate the following June, then finish his thesis by December and return to Germany.

By the third week in September, we were able to move into our housing, a beautiful duplex built by the Missionary Furlough Home Association. The duplex sat in a ring of other houses, which were all filled by furloughing missionaries. To our right, sharing the duplex, were missionaries from China;

Greek missionaries and a family who'd just returned from Kenya shared the house next door.

That's where I met Emily Moreau. With her three small girls, the youngest the same age as Tyler, it wasn't long before we found each other. They had been serving in Kenya for several years, and her husband had come to Wheaton to teach in the graduate missions department for one year.

Most afternoons, while the days were still pleasant, we sat out at the picnic table in the courtyard, letting our kids play together while we talked and got to know each other.

As I was living the "young mom with a baby" life, Dave was fully engaged in his life as a grad student. Full of excitement and enthusiasm, he came home each day with all sorts of new thoughts and ideas, as well as a stack of homework to tackle.

While grad students weren't required to be at all chapel services, he tried not to miss them, or any special speakers who came through, as he wanted to soak in as much as possible in this stimulating environment. With a young child, I didn't make it over to the campus very often, so I relied on Dave to tell me about the speakers and topics when he came home.

One afternoon, Dave arrived home and said, "You won't believe who I got to listen to today. Anita Deyneka!"

Not knowing who that was, or why he was so excited, I asked him to explain.

"She's married to Peter Deyneka, whose father, Peter Sr., started Slavic Gospel Association. Do you remember hearing about him from that speaker at the OCSC conference in Switzerland a couple years ago? He's the man who came to the

United States from Russia, got saved at Moody Church, then made trips back to Russia to share the gospel. In the 1930s he founded SGA."

I vaguely remembered the missionary who'd spoken about him. "So what did Anita have to say today?" I asked, curious.

"With the coup that happened in Russia in August, and Gorbachev resigning, she says the people of Russia are hungrier than they've ever been, and that the doors for evangelism are wide open like never before. They're getting people into the country as fast as they can, bringing Bibles and doing evangelism everywhere to take advantage of what she calls 'the hinge of history.' Nobody knows how long the doors will remain open, so they're doing all they can to penetrate with the gospel."

"And how did that impact *you*?" I asked.

He took a breath, "I think God's calling us to do something too. Something big, not just a retreat or a work project or something short-term—but longer, more permanent."

I looked at him, wide-eyed, unsure of how to respond.

"You know how we've been talking with everyone we could think of since the trip to Hungary, trying to find someone to go, live there and do ministry with the teenagers?"

I nodded. It had been a topic of many conversations over the past two years, since that first trip into Hungary.

"Well, I think *we* are the ones that God's calling to Eastern Europe, to live there and bring the gospel to young people, to disciple them and train up leaders to do the same. It's a hinge of history, like never before in our lifetime, and I think this is what God's been preparing us for all these years."

He leaned forward, grabbed my hands and asked, "So, what do you think?"

I didn't know what to say.

It was true that we'd talked about the need for someone to capture this moment of freedom, to bring the gospel into those former Communist countries. And especially to capture the hearts of young people who most likely had not heard the gospel because of the laws against "proselytizing" children.

Several generations had gone by without legally being able to invite children and teenagers to churches, meetings, camps or anything associated with Christians. Children were only allowed to go with their parents. And even then, it was risky leading your child to Christ.

Yes, the need was definitely there.

We'd heard that plenty of God's work had gone on underground during the years of Communism, but that the numbers of believers were small, especially among young people. We knew that millions of them had not even had the opportunity to hear the gospel.

Despite what I knew to be true, I spoke honestly when I said, "Do *we* need to be the ones to go? Surely there will be others who will rise to the challenge. Why would we leave a thriving ministry to go do something unknown like that?"

As I expressed those thoughts to Dave, I could see his spirit deflate for a moment. He'd come in with a fire, and I'd just dumped a bucket of ice water on him. Not to be deterred, he recovered quickly and continued on with passion as he spoke about this open door in history to reach the young people of a generation who were lost without Christ.

But it was as if my heart had turned to stone.

I had no interest in moving to another country, especially a country where they were recovering from Communism. Who knew how long freedom would last? Who knew if it would be safe? We had a family to think about. It wasn't just he and I being adventurous now.

"Dave, we have to be rational. What if Communism returns? What if it's not safe? Do you want your kids to grow up in an atheistic society? Why would we leave what we're already doing?"

Flooded with fear and a rising panic, I simply wouldn't consider his proposal.

Our conversation ended in a stalemate, neither of us willing to back down. It was an awkward evening as the elephant now sat in the room.

God's Promise
Even when you are weak in your faith, I will remain faithful
to you.
2 Timothy 2:13

CHAPTER FOURTEEN *Saying Yes*

T he next day, out at the picnic table with Emily, while the kids played on the lawn, I told her about the conversation.

"He says he thinks we are the ones called to go to Eastern Europe. How can he know that?" I asked. "I don't have any sense of that at all. Goodness, I just left my heart in Germany with our students and staff there. How can he think I could just walk away from them? I'd feel like I was betraying all of them. I couldn't give my heart somewhere else, to people I don't even know. How could he think this is something we need to do? No, I definitely don't feel called to this."

The following weeks were tense and uncomfortable between Dave and me. Any time he attempted to talk about his thoughts, he met the hardness in my heart. The longer time passed, the more I dug my heels in, not wanting to talk with him about it.

I knew Dave was praying about it, as I'd seen him on his knees in our bedroom, and I sensed that he was talking to the Lord about the situation.

To this day, I don't know what caused me to reel so far back into myself, but it wasn't pretty, and I didn't like myself as I was doing it. But I didn't know how to get out of it, except to hope Dave would change his mind and stop talking about going to Eastern Europe.

While Dave was praying about it, I wasn't. In fact, my relationship with the Lord grew stale. I found myself going through the motions of quiet times, never even getting around to prayer. It was as if I didn't want to get anywhere near God, afraid he was going to rope me into Dave's plan, and there would be no escape.

One evening after dinner, which had been animated only because of Tyler's antics, Dave asked if we could talk. I mumbled yes, knowing what the topic of conversation was going to be, though I wanted to avoid it. Dave had been quiet all week, not saying anything about it; I knew this was going to be another attempt to convince me.

Once Tyler was in bed, we sat together on the couch: me on one end, Dave on the other. "Can you come over here?" Dave asked, trying to make it playful, though I knew there was pain behind that request.

I moved a little closer.

"Listen, I know it's been difficult between us these past few weeks. And I'm really sorry I put you on the defense. That wasn't right of me. I shouldn't have come on so strong. Will you forgive me for that?"

This stunned me. It wasn't at all what I was expecting. I nodded, quietly answering yes.

He continued, "I don't ever want to be separated from you, physically or emotionally. If we're not one flesh, we're not living

the way God wants us to. These past weeks have been miserable, and I take responsibility for that."

"As I've been praying about it …"

Oh, no, here it comes, another plea for me to join him in this crazy idea.

"… I realized that I went about this the wrong way. God wouldn't call me without calling you too …"

Really?

"… So I committed to praying and trusting God. I realize that if he is calling me to do something in Eastern Europe, he will call you too … I don't have to try and convince you. We're one flesh, and I'm not going to live a separate life from you … we said we'd live life as a whole, not fragmented …

"… Whatever time it takes, I'm going to trust God to move in your heart one way or the other. When you're sure of what he's saying to you about this, then we can talk about it. Until then, I'm just going to pray, and it would be great if you did too, so that we both know what he's saying. I won't bring it up again until you let me know that you've heard from God. Will you join me in praying about it?"

I'd been ready to defend my position, and he'd just called a truce.

While I still felt sure that God was never going to ask me to do this, I told him yes, I would pray about it. And I meant it.

It was a relief to close the gap between us and get back to living close again. I felt a sense of hope that we were going to get through this difficult time. I also thought that in the end, we'd head back to Germany and continue on with Malachi.

Through Thanksgiving, while having a reunion with our Karlsruhe youth group kids who'd come to see us in Wheaton from colleges around the country, we lived peacefully together without the tension of the past weeks. It was a joyous time with our students as we ate meals together, reminisced and caught up on everyone's lives.

Shortly afterward, newly engaged Dan Hash (a Malachi staff member) and Laura Larrabee came to see us. After a broken engagement between them a year and a half prior, it was so good to see them happily together, moving toward marriage the coming summer.

As we discussed the future, talk quickly turned to the events that had taken place that fall in Russia and Eastern Europe. The three of them began dreaming aloud about what it would be like to do ministry there, sharing the gospel, doing discipleship and training young leaders.

Although I was praying about God's calling on our lives, I wasn't anywhere near ready to talk about plans, so didn't join in. This saddened me. But I also couldn't pretend to be somewhere that I wasn't, so I listened as they bantered about thoughts and dreams of the future there.

True to his word, Dave didn't engage me in the conversation, nor bring it up again after they left. We were back to relating well in every other area of life, with just that one area walled off with a "Do Not Disturb" sign hanging on it. And we both just let it be there.

With Dave's family in Germany for Christmas, we made plans to go to Washington to be with mine. A change of job for my dad had sent them to the Seattle area, where they

were now living in the town of Issaquah. We were excited to see the city and experience a new part of the Northwest for Christmas.

It was also the first Christmas with my parents since I'd left for Europe in 1986. For the first time in five years, not only were they having their daughter and son-in-law home, but their new grandson as well. They couldn't have been more pleased.

"If you two would like to take a night and go somewhere, we'd be happy to keep Tyler," my mom and dad offered shortly after we arrived. It didn't take long for us to take them up on that. We headed out the next afternoon, off to Puget Sound to find a place to stay for the night.

We stopped along the way to sightsee and shop, and then arrived in Port Townsend around dinnertime. There weren't many choices within our budget, so it was easy to choose a local motel where we quickly checked in and went to find a place for dinner.

Conversation was easy, food was cheap and we were happy. The tension of the past months had dissipated, and it had been weeks since we'd spoken about Eastern Europe. Although I'd prayed about it, I had yet to hear anything from God, so planned to tell Dave soon that I didn't sense his calling. It was my hope that this idea could finally be put to rest.

Back in our motel room, we turned on the TV to watch Olympic gymnastics trials in preparation for the upcoming summer games. I'd always enjoyed watching gymnastics, so it was a pleasant way to spend the evening.

Asking if I wanted anything, Dave said he was going to the vending machine to get drinks and ice. I told him I'd

love a Coke, and off he went with the plastic ice bucket in his hands.

Suddenly, within the space of a few brief minutes, something of profound significance occurred.

With my eyes on the screen, watching young Romanian gymnasts perform, I heard God speak to my heart. It was so clear, I was sure in that moment that it was *him*.

"Connie, do you see those girls?" he gently whispered into my heart, guiding me to look more intently at their faces on the screen.

"Do you think you would love those girls any less than you love your girls in Germany? Look closely in their faces . . . what do you see? Do you see girls who need to know me? They need me just as much as your girls in Germany do."

My heart beating wildly, tears in my eyes, I listened intently.

"If you'll say yes to where I'm leading, I'll bring many girls into your life in Eastern Europe, ones who you will love deeply. You'll tell them about me. You'll share life together. You'll see my kingdom come as you watch me transform their lives. And as I lead you there, I'll take care of you."

My heart is pounding as I type those words, just as it did that night in Port Townsend, Washington.

He had spoken. It was completely clear.

My perspective was utterly changed in a moment.

Stunned, I sat on the bed, realizing he had just broken through and called me to a new life in a most personal way. It was gentle and loving. There was nothing forced about it. And he completely melted my heart of stone.

Dave walked back into the motel room a moment later. Before he could sit down, while he was still standing with a bucket of ice and two drinks in his hand, I spoke.

"Do you want to talk about going to Eastern Europe?"

God's Promise
I am able to do more than you could possibly imagine.
Ephesians 3:20

CHAPTER FIFTEEN

Catching the Vision

I love that God didn't paint a big sweeping picture, or roll out for me the next twenty years of his plan. Instead, he showed me the faces of girls and reminded me that he loved them, and that I would too.

Dave and I stayed up late that night in our motel room, talking about all the things we hadn't been able to talk about until then.

"So what exactly did you have in mind?" I asked while sipping on the Coke he'd brought from the vending machine.

Bursting out in laughter, he replied, "No, I want to know what *you* had in mind and what caused you to lock up like that!"

I didn't take offense. He was right. I'd been completely locked up.

But now I was free! Free to dream, free to ask questions, free to explore.

"Well, you really want to know what was in my mind?" I asked in sincerity. "I pictured us moving to a village somewhere in the middle of Eastern Europe, with dirt roads, no stores, unstable electricity and not many people living in the village. I envisioned houses that are tiny, with dirt floors. There are old grandmas with scarves over their heads, chasing chickens outside our door as they lean over their canes."

I added, "I see myself alone, inside our house with a bunch of kids, while you're off saving the world somewhere else."

"Really?" he asked in utter amazement. I took that to mean it wasn't what he had in mind. "You thought we'd go alone? That isn't what I had in mind at all! I would never go in without a team. We built a team to reach students in Germany, and that's what I hope to do again in Eastern Europe. In fact, let's make a list right now of who we'd like to go with us, if God called them too."

Taking out his black notebook, I began to write down the names of our friends: Dan and Laura, Ken and Andrea, Jim and Lina, Greg … all people we'd worked with in Malachi, whom we loved and thought might have a heart to reach these young people.

"Okay, let's make another list," Dave offered. "Let's write down what we would need and want in a home, wherever it is that God might lead us."

In the same black notebook, I made a list: space for guests, rooms for children, a big enough living room to have meetings and gatherings, a yard, neighbors, easy for people to get to, close to a grocery store, and even a dishwasher (I'd never had one before, so decided to throw that one into the mix).

The longer we talked into the night, the more excited I became. Dave's vision was not a small one; he wanted to reach hundreds of thousands of young people with the gospel in the former Communist nations. It seemed impossible, and we didn't know how God would accomplish that vision. But we were now in it together.

We dreamed about what country we would live in that night. We prayed for the young people of Eastern Europe, like the Romanian girls I'd seen on TV. We thought about teammates who would join us. And we glimpsed our first vision of what it would be like to reach the youth of Eastern Europe for Jesus.

It was a night neither one of us anticipated, but a night we'd never forget.

My heart was bursting with gratefulness to the Lord for his patience with me over the past months, and I committed again to following him wherever he led us.

After we returned to Wheaton, Dave continued his heavy load of studies. Week after week professors, fellow students, studies and time spent in God's Word impacted him. All of this was fuel for our continuing thoughts about ministry in Eastern Europe.

By springtime, we'd talked with Dan and Laura, and Ken and Andrea, two of the couples on our list, about joining us in this new venture to the unknown. Despite few details or concrete plans, they were on board and committed to seeing where God would lead all of us.

As we talked about next steps, Dave said he felt the need to spend time in fasting and prayer for the future. Best told

in his words, Dave describes what happened during his time away:

> When God's people didn't know what to do, they sought him in fasting and prayer, expecting he would speak. So I set aside two days and went to a lake in southern Wisconsin. "I'm just going to be with you, Lord," I said to him. "I want to hear your voice. I am listening for your plans about how to reach young people with the gospel in Eastern Europe."
>
> The first day I opened my Bible and said, "Okay, God, what do you want to say to me?" But God didn't say what I expected. I was asking him, "What about the future, what do you want to do?"
>
> But he said, "What about the present? What are you doing about some areas in your life?"
>
> That whole day it was like God took me to the woodshed. The Lord said, "Dave, if you want to be used, you've got to become more usable."
>
> He spent the whole day showing me my sin. I spent the day in repentance.
>
> The next day I pulled my chair to the edge of the lake and said, "Okay, God, I've confessed everything I can. With my heart clean and yielded to you, will you tell me something about the future?"
>
> God then started speaking. It wasn't an audible voice, but maybe you've experienced one of those times where you know, "God's talking to me right now."

After listening to him speak, I took out my notebook and wrote this at the top of the page: "A movement of God among the youth of Eastern Europe that finds its home in the local church and transforms society."

Then I started dreaming. What would that look like? How would we do it? What would it be like to be a part of such a vision? A vision where whole countries would be different: Poland would be different, Romania would be different and Czechoslovakia would be different, all because God would do something special among a generation of young people as he called them to himself.

Then I said, "God, what do you specifically want us to do?"

I listened, and then wrote this down: "Equip young leaders to fulfill Christ's commission through the local church."

And that day, the vision for a ministry to young people in Eastern Europe was born.

God brought to Dave's mind the story of King Josiah. He was just eight years old when he became king, and then at sixteen something significant began to happen.

In the eighth year of his reign, he started "seeking the God of his father, David." But his father wasn't David. His father was Amon, a wicked, evil king, and his grandfather, Manasseh, was said to be even more wicked than all the kings around him.

Josiah skipped his father and grandfather and sought after the God of his ancestor, David. He began to rebuild the temple, and in doing so, found the Law that had been lost. He read it, tore his robe and repented, not only for himself, but also on behalf of his people.

Immediately, he called the people together, read the book of the law out loud in their presence and called them to repentance as well. He marched out and began tearing down idols in the land that had been there since the days of Solomon. He was the first king to cleanse the land of idols.

Our vision became one of thinking about and praying for the young "Josiahs" in Eastern Europe. We believed God for young people like King Josiah, who would hear the gospel, respond in repentance, lead the way for others and change whole countries for God's sake and his kingdom.

This became our passion, focus and vision as we moved forward with the ministry of "Josiah Venture."

God's Promise
I will be the voice behind you, guiding you in the way you
should go.
Isaiah 30:21

CHAPTER SIXTEEN

First Impressions

S hortly after Dave's significant time in Wisconsin, another important event made its way into our lives: we were pregnant with baby number two.

Dave walked through graduation in May, having completed all his coursework, and then set to work on writing his thesis over the next months. While he was hard at work, Tyler and I headed to my parents' house near Seattle for a visit and then stayed busy with friends in the Wheaton area through the end of the summer.

On a hot July day in Wheaton, I went in for a checkup. We found out we were expecting another boy! I loved thinking about Tyler having a brother, and started praying for them and the kind of relationship they would have in the years to come. It gave me no end of delight to know these would be the two who would begin life with us in Eastern Europe, wherever that would be.

In the basement of a friend's house where we stayed for the summer, Dave worked day and night to finish his thesis, turning in his work on "The Five Stages of Development: Spiritual Growth in Adolescence" just as the summer semester ended. While it went for review, we left for a cross-country trip to visit churches, friends, supporters and our families.

After two months on the road, sharing our new vision, we arrived back in Chicago for one last review and the acceptance of his thesis. With that completed, we flew home to Germany in November 1992 to begin preparation for our move into Eastern Europe.

While away, we'd sublet the apartment that Dave and I had lived in prior to leaving, so were able to come home to all of our things and begin to make a place for Caleb, our soon-to-be born baby boy.

But within a week of our arrival, I began to have contractions. Two months too soon.

It was a gift from the Lord that this hadn't happened earlier. We'd prayed throughout our cross-country trip, knowing there was a chance of pre-term labor happening again. When it didn't, we were grateful, and expected the rest of the pregnancy to proceed without complication.

It didn't.

Doctor Stork put me on strict bed rest until Christmas, which would bring Caleb to thirty-six weeks in the pregnancy. She hoped by then he would be developed enough that she could take me off the medication and bed rest, and let him come.

It was one thing to be in bed when I didn't have any children. It was a whole different story to have a lively two-year-old

and be in bed all day. Dave, his mom and our friends helped out when they could, but Tyler and I spent a lot of time reading books during the next four weeks.

With the news that I'd be taken off bed rest and medication the day after Christmas, we knew Caleb's birth was imminent, so asked my mom to come as soon as possible.

She arrived the morning of December 27, and we all breathed a sigh of relief when Dave brought her back from the Frankfurt airport. Caleb could come any time now.

But the New Year came and went. We shopped and cooked, played with Tyler and even did a 10-kilometer "*Volksmarch*" in a town nearby.

Finally at 5 a.m. on January 20, four weeks after I'd been taken off bed rest, it was time to go to the hospital. After eight hours of labor, I delivered a healthy boy.

However, while watching them weigh and measure Caleb, I began to feel lightheaded. I remember trying to talk to get someone's attention, but had no energy to raise my voice. A nurse glanced over at me and suddenly a flurry of activity commenced in the delivery room. They handed Dave his new son, rushed him out with no explanation and within minutes, I was put under anesthesia.

When Caleb came through the birth canal, extensive tearing occurred, and I began to bleed profusely. By the time they caught what had happened, they estimated that I'd already lost two-thirds of my blood. Thankfully, their quick action saved my life.

My mom was such a help in those days, as well as when we came home ten days later. I've always been so grateful for both

my parents' sacrifices for me, but never more so than at this time. While my dad was home in the States, my mom stayed seven weeks to make sure I could function on my own.

Within two weeks, I had color back in my cheeks, and was feeling better. After several visits, the doctor declared that my body had produced its own blood to make up for what I'd lost, so I never needed additional blood. Our hearts rejoiced in God's protection over me, and we were thankful to be on the other side of Caleb's birth.

My mom's help during this time was invaluable. Looking for a way to bless her for all she'd done, we asked if there was anything she'd like to do before leaving. She said she'd like to go to the Czech Republic.

This was one of the countries we were considering moving into to begin Josiah Venture, but I'd never been there, so was anxious to see it. I knew it would be a while before I could make the trip without additional help, so when my mom asked to go, I jumped at the chance.

It was surreal to cross the border into Czech, which was, as a country, only six weeks old. On January 1, 1993, the "Velvet Divorce" had taken place. Now instead of Czechoslovakia, there was the Czech Republic and Slovakia. They had amicably split from each other, separate for the first time since World War II.

Driving across the border and into the countryside for the first time, I was deeply aware of the fact that I had roots there. My great-grandparents on my dad's side had immigrated to the United States back in the late 1800s from this very land we were now driving through. My great-grandmother was from Prague, great-grandfather from Plzeň. They met and married after they

both arrived in the United States, and I'd grown up proud of the fact that I was a quarter "Bohemian."

But as we drove through the country, I began to feel uncomfortable. The foreignness of the land hit immediately as we began traveling through it. Road signs were unreadable. People's faces were drawn and closed. Stores were not what I was used to. There were no quick, easy places to stop for a meal. And it was dark, gloomy, cold, and smoggy as we drove into the capital, Prague.

The former dean of men at Multnomah Bible College Barry Keiser and his wife, Jean, were living in Prague at that time. They graciously made space for all of us in their high-rise apartment on the outskirts of the city until we could find a hotel.

Armed with maps and instructions on how to get downtown, we made our way to the center, excited to see the city we'd heard so much about.

But it was oddly empty as we walked into the heart of the city to Václavské náměstí (Wenceslas Square). In November 1989, during the Velvet Revolution, large demonstrations with hundreds of thousands of people were held in that very place. Yet on this day it was quiet, with few people on the street.

In a shop, while we were browsing the famous Bohemia crystal, a woman ventured to speak to us in English. "You are from the United States?"

Too difficult to explain that Dave, the kids and I lived in Germany, but that my mom was from there, we merely replied, "Yes, we are. And you have a beautiful city. We're enjoying it very much."

"Yes, it is beautiful, but not today. You have not heard the news? The air is very bad. Schools are closed so children will

stay inside. It is a very bad … what do you call it? Inversion? You should not have your children outside in this terrible air."

Now we understood why there were few people on the streets. But with only one day to see the city, we decided to brave the damp air with the heavy smell of coal, and continue through the streets of Prague.

With Dave carrying baby Caleb in a front pack, inside his jacket, I pushed Tyler's stroller through the cobblestoned streets as we, along with my mom, took in famous sites such as Old Town Square, the Charles Bridge and Prague castle.

Despite dreary skies, dirty buildings covered in coal dust and dampness in the air, we began to fall in love with Prague. Its old-world charm shone through the grime and decay. While people were not overly friendly, they were kind, and we felt drawn to them.

"I don't know if I could live in this big of a city, but I'm beginning to like it here," I remember saying to Dave later that night. "There's something that draws me, maybe my roots?" I ventured.

Over the next months, Dave, along with Ken Pitcher, traveled throughout Central and Eastern Europe, meeting with Christian leaders and seeking God's will for where we were to settle.

They were also searching for someone who was from one of these countries, who shared our passion and vision for reaching their young people, and who would have time and energy to invest with us in doing so.

By mid-May they had identified a potential partner in the Czech Republic and in Poland. We made plans to visit both places, along with Ken, and his wife, Andrea, to continue narrowing down our possibilities of a location to begin the work of Josiah Venture, and define where each of the three couples, including Dan and Laura Hash, would live and serve.

Driving into the Czech Republic in the spring was a completely different experience than when we'd been there in the middle of winter. Flowers were bursting forth, trees were covered in blossoms, and fields were bright green with new growth. The countryside was stunningly beautiful.

As we drove, Dave explained that we would first travel to Havířov, a city on the outskirts of Ostrava, the third-largest city in the country. This was one of the potential places for us to live, and he wanted me to meet the couple he'd identified as ones who shared a similar heart and vision for reaching young people.

As we drove toward Havířov, the small, quaint villages along the two-lane roads captivated me. I felt excitement growing in my heart as we crested a hill that would drop us down into the heart of the city. This could be my new home!

But as we made our way down the central boulevard, past rows and rows of apartment buildings, my heart began to sink. The buildings looked old, many covered in graffiti. The yards in front were unkempt, with grass and weeds growing wildly.

Children's play equipment in courtyards of apartment buildings looked as if it had been deserted long ago, the paint peeling off and parts broken. Sandboxes sat empty, with tall grass grown up around the sides.

It was a dismal sight.

We arrived in the center of town and parked. Getting out of the car onto the broken sidewalk, my heart sank. *This is where Dave thinks we should live?* I didn't know if I could do it.

Walking into a grocery store nearby, I tried to imagine what I could feed my family if we lived there. The fresh produce section had mostly potatoes, cabbage and cauliflower, while the aisles were filled with tin cans, including something that looked like a meat product I would not be inclined to eat. A bottle of Heinz ketchup and a box of Uncle Ben's rice heartened me momentarily, but not enough to give me hope for our future there.

None too soon, we left the store and headed to the home of Vladek and Jana Lipus. This was the couple we'd come to see and talk with about the possibility of joining our vision to reach the young people in this country.

We entered their apartment and were met with warm hugs and a bounty of food on their coffee table. I began to relax. Their kindness overwhelmed me in the coming hours as Jana brought in trays of more food, and Vladek spoke English, telling us stories of how he'd come to Christ and what it was like living in a Communist country as a Christian.

The couple had five children ranging in age from two to sixteen. Lucy, the oldest, also spoke English. She and her siblings entertained Tyler and Caleb, while we adults talked into the night.

When it came time for bed, Vladek and Jana gave the four of us their bedroom, which was also the living room.

I hadn't noticed, but there was a bed on the other side of the seating area where we'd spent the evening. They made up a small bed on the floor for Tyler, and we set up Caleb's portable crib nearby and slept comfortably through the night.

I'm sure Vladek and Jana were not as comfortable as we were. They must have slept in one of the two bedrooms that the five children were in. I was overwhelmed by their sacrifice and generosity. But still, a feeling of unsettledness covered me. As we left the next morning to drive over the border to Poland, I again wondered how it would feel to live here.

Crossing the border from the town of Český Těšín into Poland, I began to relax. The countryside looked much cleaner and less run-down. As we drove into the small resort town of Ustroń, despite the futuristic pyramid-shaped hotels on the mountainside, I thought, "I like it here much better!" I hoped that the meeting would go well, and that Dave would lean toward us moving to Poland.

Over a meal of pierogi, the famous Polish dish of boiled pockets of dough stuffed with potato, sauerkraut and ground meat, we talked for several hours with Vacek, the young man we'd met there, to talk about a partnership for reaching Polish young people with the gospel.

While he was a wonderful man with a passion for Christ and reaching his country, I sensed that we weren't connecting with him in the same way we had with Vladek the night before. I couldn't help but think how Dan and Laura would enjoy and connect with him more than us.

As we drove back to Czech that afternoon, I wondered how this was going to turn out.

God's Promise
Ask me for wisdom and I will generously give it to you.
James 1:5

 *Making the Move*

Within a few weeks of our visits to Czech and Poland, the Lord confirmed that we and the Pitchers were to base in the Czech Republic, and that it was a better fit for Dan and Laura to go to Poland.

With so many details to take into consideration, how I'd felt in Havířov was low on the priority list. Although at the time it wasn't someplace I would've chosen by the looks of it, the connection we had with the Lipus family was the key.

Vladek had already been working secretly with youth under Communism, and shared our heart for reaching the young people of his city and his country. So it was determined that we would move to Havířov, the Pitchers would move to Ostrava, and Dan and Laura would move to Ustroń in Poland.

We traveled to the States that summer to meet with our new mission organization that would house the small Josiah Venture team, and to update the pastor and elders at Grace Church of

DuPage. Up until this point, Grace Church, pastored by Rich Kerns, was the church we'd attended while Dave worked on his master's degree, but was not a supporting church. Yet after Rich mentored Dave during our time in Wheaton, he felt we needed Grace as another church partner before beginning this new ministry.

They had a commissioning service for us before we returned to Germany, committing both financial and prayer support that we'd need to begin Josiah Venture.

While we were in the States sharing the vision, Vladek had spent several months looking for potential places for us to live in Havířov. He contacted Dave in August after we'd returned to Germany. "I've found two places that are for sale. Could you come to look at them?" Vladek asked.

With the boys recovering from the chicken pox, we left them with Dave's sister Joyce and her husband, David Schroeder (the same David who auditioned me for Malachi!), who were living in Darmstadt, Germany, at the time. David had taken the role of Malachi director when we left for Wheaton two years prior, and had continued in that role after it became clear we were being called elsewhere.

After dropping off the boys, we began the eleven-hour drive to Havířov. Crossing the border this time, we knew the Czech Republic would be our home, so looked at it with different eyes. We prayed as we drove that God would do something far more than we could ever imagine with the tiny mustard seed of faith we were starting with.

Early the next morning, after spending the night at Vladek and Jana's, we headed out to look at the two possibilities

of homes for us. The first was in a large housing area at the north end of the city called Šumbark. It was an apartment in a *Paneláky*, high-rise buildings that had been constructed under Communism.

My heart sank as we walked through it.

Looking out the windows at dozens of *panalaky*, with only small patches of grass as potential play places, I couldn't imagine raising our family there. It seemed bleak and uninviting.

But when Vladek explained that there were very few apartments for sale, and even fewer homes, I tried to adjust my expectations and surrender to the Lord's plan for our family.

As we crossed to the other side of the city to see a house that was for sale, I didn't hold out much hope that it would be right for us and assumed we'd be making that apartment our home.

As we made a right-hand turn onto a road, and bumped all the way down to the end of it, Vladek said, "This is the only house for sale in the city. I know it doesn't look like much, but maybe you could do some renovation on it."

We got out onto a muddy driveway, with a dilapidated fence on either side, and looked up at the only house for sale in a city of ninety thousand people. A large man, with his belly protruding from underneath a dirty white T-shirt, met us at the door. Vladek translated as we began to tour the house.

"I built this house myself," the man proudly stated as we walked through small rooms with uneven floors, worn fixtures and mismatched doors. "I've also got a chicken coop and a shed for the pigs outside."

My eyes were wide, as I tried to imagine us living there. Especially when he opened a door and there was an entire slab

of meat hanging from a hook. *Would I have to do that too?* I wondered. I shuddered at the thought.

After touring the house, his meek wife brought coffee as we sat down in the living room to talk. Not knowing how coffee was brewed there at the time, I took my first sip and felt grounds in my teeth as I drank. Turkish coffee. You're supposed to let it settle before you take a drink.

Through translation we found out that he lived in this house with his wife, son, daughter-in-law, grandson and mother. The son no longer wanted to live there, so they needed to sell it in order to buy two separate apartments to live in.

After politely saying thank you for their hospitality, we returned to Vladek's place with a big decision to make. Dave and I took a walk through the city that afternoon, discussing the pros and cons of each that we'd seen. The cons seemed to outweigh the pros for both the apartment and the house we'd looked it, and it was hard to get excited about either one.

But as we stood on the corner across the street from the sports stadium, Dave said, "I think we need to take the house. It's got the most potential of the two. And while I can't promise it will be your dream house, I'll do everything I can to make it livable and comfortable for you. What do you think?"

Knowing in my heart that he was right, and that at least we'd have a yard for the boys to play in, we went back to Vladek and told him to proceed with purchasing the house.

Dave traveled into Czech a month later with thousands of dollars in cash at the bottom of a diaper wipe box, the money wrapped in plastic with wipes on top to disguise it. At that time there was no way to do an international bank transfer

of funds, so this was the only option available to pay for the house.

By the end of October 1993, we'd bought a house in Havířov.

The weeks that followed were like a dream. Were we really moving to the Czech Republic? Did we really buy a house there? Was our dream of reaching young people in Eastern Europe really attainable?

These questions and so many more swirled through my head as I purged and packed until one day everything was done and our apartment was empty.

Sitting amid the last of the things to be loaded onto the truck, I felt the tears come.

We were finally saying goodbye to our life in Germany, to the ministry I'd first come to nearly ten years earlier. We were saying goodbye to our staff and friends, and to our family who lived there: Dave's parents, and his sister and her family, which now included my niece and nephew.

It was a bittersweet moment. I knew that God had called us to where we were going. But it was hard to say goodbye to where we'd been. My heart felt torn in two that day as the last of our belongings were packed into the truck, and we turned the key in the door for the last time and walked away.

Dan and Laura had arrived in Germany by this time, and the plan was for them to drive with the boys and me, while Dave went a few days earlier with the truck that held our belongings. He knew it would be a long wait through customs at the border, so didn't want to put us through that. I was grateful.

Friends in St. Leon let us stay with them for our last three days in Germany, showering us with love and last-minute gifts

of food from the commissary and toys from the PX for the boys as we faced the long trip in front of us.

Finally, on November 9, 1993, Dan and Laura arrived to meet us, we said our last goodbyes, put everything and everybody in two cars and headed toward the former Communist countries where we were planning to live.

Having made a ten-year commitment, each of the three couples knew this was no small task ahead of us. Though we couldn't envision what kinds of roadblocks and difficulties we would encounter, we knew that we would stay for the long haul and endure whatever came our way.

And it was all because of this vision:

A movement of God among the youth of Eastern Europe that finds its home in the local church and transforms society.

That's what we were committing ourselves to as we sped down the autobahn, headed for our new homes.

Laura rode with the boys and me for most of the trip, while Dan led in the car in front of us. Tyler was almost three and a half, while Caleb was not even ten months old, so I needed help making that long trip with such little guys. At 10 p.m., we drove down the long hill into Havířov, heading toward our house and our new life.

My legs were shaking beneath the steering wheel as I made the turn onto U Zborůvky, our new street. With both wild excitement and looming fear, I made the last turn and came to a stop in front of the garage where we'd been just months before as we looked up at the house.

But now, this was *our* house. And I was here to stay, for a long time.

With a great deal of nervousness, I began to unbuckle the boys from their car seats. Dave came out to meet us, embracing the boys and me before leading us to the front door. Lucy, Vladek's sixteen-year-old daughter, had left a sign there to greet us: "Welcome to the world where dreams come true."

I hoped with all my heart that would happen.

Cakes and sandwiches, lovingly prepared by Jana, were inside the house, so after coats came off, we sat amid boxes and ate as Dan, Laura and I recalled our trip, and then heard about Dave's coming across the border with all our belongings. Although there had been some tense moments with paperwork and documents, he had been able to make the crossing and arrived to a whole team of people from our new church to help unload the truck.

As I walked around the bottom floor of our house where boxes were stacked to the ceiling, and furniture and furnishings were stashed everywhere, reality set in. *This is where we'll live!* I thought to myself. *Memories we can't even begin to anticipate will happen right here.*

Plans were already in motion for renovations on the second floor, which would be our main living area. We walked upstairs to the emptiness of those rooms and stood at the windows looking out at what was now our view into life.

While Dan and Dave looked around, Laura and I stood in the semi-darkness, with Caleb on my hip, Tyler clinging to my side while the light of one dull light bulb in the hallway dimly lit us.

And then it happened. God met me there, much as he had in Port Townsend two years earlier. But he didn't speak. Instead, he showed me a film in the depths of my mind. It was as if the projector fast-forwarded, and we were no longer in our first night together in our house, but rather, in the future. In this supernatural film, Tyler stood on one side of me, Caleb on the other. Both boys were tall and looked to be in their late twenties. We were looking out that very window, reminiscing about our life there.

"Hasn't it been great, Mom?" one of them said.

"I loved living here. I'm sad to see us go," the other one added.

As if a bystander, I looked at myself, aged but content as I stood between my boys. I could tell that the thought resting in my heart was a good one by the look on my face. "It's been a really good life, hasn't it, boys?" I asked without expecting an answer. "God met us here in ways I never could've imagined. I'm sad to leave too."

In a flicker, the scene was gone, and I was back to holding Caleb and feeling Tyler leaning against me. The film had passed before my eyes as real as if it had just happened, and yet here I was at the very beginning, the first night, with a whole lot of life to live before we'd ever reach a scene like that.

Grateful to the Lord for the gift of that moment, I left the room with a supernatural peace in my heart that can only be explained by God's presence. Somehow I knew that this would be a good life, and that we'd be okay, no matter what happened.

God had led us there. We had followed his plan. He would see us through each and every day of our life there.

God's Promise
All my plans will be fulfilled, for I know the end from
the beginning.
Isaiah 46:10

CHAPTER EIGHTEEN

A Providential Misunderstanding

The weeks and months following that first night were full of transition and adaptation.

Absolutely everything was new. We couldn't yet speak the language; everyday things were a challenge. Finding groceries and items for the house took hours of our day. Hunting down necessary items for the renovation upstairs became a challenging game for Dave as he tracked down every hardware store in the city, searching for what was needed.

With the help of Vladek and others, the renovations were completed by Christmas, and we moved upstairs just two days before the holiday. In my kitchen was the one thing I had dared to ask for that night we were in Puget Sound, when God had spoken so clearly to me. It wasn't pretty, as it was a castoff from a military sale, but I had a working dishwasher.

God was so kind to me.

After the holidays, Vladek's daughter Lucy moved into our house to begin helping us learn the Czech language. We were determined to go after it and learn it well, though we'd heard how difficult a language it was.

Dave met with a tutor three times a week, spending at least twenty hours a week working on language in those early days. Lucy would drill him at home in the evenings, working on vocabulary expansion, as well as the dreaded grammar of a Slavic language.

My tutor was our pastor's mother. She had come to Christ shortly after Communism began, and faithfully lived for him during the hard years that followed. She was my first window into the hearts and lives of Czechs and taught me more than language; she taught me history and told stories so that I'd understand the heart and background of the Czech people.

Though language learning was overwhelming at times due to the enormity of the task, those were precious days of learning from her.

Near the end of January, Lucy was with me in the kitchen one afternoon as I prepared dinner. Vibrant, vivacious and energetic, she brought a lot of joy to our lives each day. She helped with language, the boys, the house and was a friend to me, even though there was such an age difference.

"Hey, you should come to my school and talk to my principal about teaching English there," she remarked that afternoon.

"Oh, Lucy, I can't do that! I've got the boys, I'm trying to learn the language and everything is so new. I couldn't add one more thing to my plate—especially teaching," I answered.

And I meant it. Life was good, but overwhelming, as I tried to process everything I was taking in each day.

However, she persisted, "You should just come and talk to him—see what it's like."

I dismissed her suggestion with a wave of my hand and a laugh at the outrageousness of her request. I wouldn't do that in a million years.

The next day she came home from school and said, "Hey, I talked to my principal. He said you can come in tomorrow morning and meet him at eight, and I'll translate for you."

What? I thought I'd made it clear that I couldn't do that.

Later on that evening, when I explained the prospect to Dave, he replied, "Well, I don't know how you can get out of it now. Why don't you just go, gather information and find out what the school is like. Of course you're not going to take a job, but maybe it'd be good to just have a foot in the door by meeting him. We do want to get into the high school at some point to reach those students."

So the next morning I drove Lucy to school. I was nervous. Not really sure why I was even there, I didn't know if I should be asking him questions, or letting him ask me. I chose the latter.

He was warm and communicative as Lucy translated his questions and my answers. When we left, I was relieved, but glad I'd met with him. Getting into that high school to meet students and share Jesus with them was definitely one of our priorities, so it was good to have made a first step in that direction.

Back at home, Dave asked me how it went and I said, "Well, it was definitely interesting and fun to see lots of high school students. But I'm sure not going to teach there. I thanked him

for his time and told him I wouldn't be able to do anything at the school for now."

Dave went downstairs to study Czech, and I moved on with my day.

Later that afternoon I heard the door downstairs slam, which meant Lucy was home. Seconds later I heard her bound up the stairs, calling out, "Connie! Connie!"

"I'm in here giving lunch to the boys," I replied.

Screeching to a halt at the kitchen door, she squealed, "You got the job!"

"What job?" I asked, my heart starting to pound.

"The one my principal offered you today!"

"But I didn't know there was a job, and I sure didn't say I'd take it," I said, pushing my chair back from the table. "You know I can't teach at your school."

Lucy's face fell. "But you have to," she said desperately.

"Lucy, I can't take that job. You'll just have to tell him there was some kind of misunderstanding and that I was merely making polite conversation with him when we talked today. Really, I can't do it," I said as I wiped peanut butter off Caleb's face.

"You don't understand, Connie," she persisted. "When he found out that you could take the job, he fired the other English teacher today. So you have to come be our teacher."

"What?" I asked incredulously. "What do you mean?"

"Well, he'd been looking for a reason to fire the American guy who's been teaching us. But without any other option, he hadn't been able to. He was really excited about you so he could get rid of that guy. He's been a problem in the school. You'll be so much better! Oh, and you start next Monday," she said with a hopeful, sheepish look on her face.

Little did I know that I'd subtly been offered a job that morning, and had subtly accepted one.

What could I do now?

Dave was not happy later on that afternoon when he heard what had happened. "I thought you told him you weren't interested," said Dave, frustrated.

"That's what I thought too. I don't know what happened. I really thought I made it clear that I wasn't available to teach," I quietly offered.

"Well, you must've said something that made him think you were," he answered, uncharacteristically terse.

He found Lucy in her room and said, "Lucy, there's been a mistake. You're just going to have to tell your principal that Connie can't teach, that she's sorry, and maybe she can do it some other time."

Heartbroken, she replied, "I really can't do that, Dave. He knows Connie is a Christian, and if I tell him no, I don't know if you'll ever be able to get into the high school. It would ruin your reputation if she doesn't come to teach."

At a stalemate, Dave came back out into the living room and asked me again, "Why did you take that job?"

It was tense around our house for the next few days.

Finally, three days after I'd been hired, having sent no word back to the principal yet, Dave and I sat down in the living room after the boys had gone to bed.

"I'm really not happy about this situation," Dave said. "Teaching English honestly seems like a waste of time. We came

here to learn the language and minister in it. If you take the job, it will mean less time for both of us to learn the language. And, if you take it, I'll have to stay home with the boys. You know I love them and don't ever mind watching them, but it just doesn't fit with the plan for you to work and me to be at home with them."

The vision from God to reach the youth of Eastern Europe was burning in his heart. He didn't want to be deterred from it.

"The only solution I can see is that I take this job for you. But I'm not very happy about that," he said.

It was silent for a while as we both digested this suggestion.

Then I quietly said, "You know, Dave, I really think God is in this."

"You're saying that because I'm taking the job for you," Dave quietly replied.

"No, I think maybe we're going to look back someday and see this was really important."

I hoped I was right.

Promise of God
Nothing will be impossible for those who have even a little faith.
Matthew 17:19-20

CHAPTER NINETEEN

Not Expected

The next Monday morning, Dave showed up in the principal's office. "I'm here to take my wife's place as a teacher in your English department," he stated.

"Well, do you have a degree to teach English?" the principal asked through Lucy, who was there to translate.

"I have my master's degree in education, and I've been speaking English all my life," Dave offered.

"I'll need to have a copy of your diploma for my records, but I guess that will do," said the principal.

"What exactly do you want me to do here?" Dave then asked.

"I have teachers who teach the students grammar. What I need from you is to get the students talking. They need to practice their English with a native speaker if they're going to become proficient at it. You can talk about holidays, sports, family, jobs—pretty much any topic, as long as you do it in English."

Something clicked in Dave's mind.

"I'll be honest with you," said Dave. "I'm a pastor, and I came here to train youth pastors and work with teenagers. If you say I can talk about any topic, would it be possible to talk with your students about God during class?"

The principal sat back in his chair and thought for a moment. "Well, if you do it in English, yes, I guess that would be okay."

What an open door! This news gave Dave the encouragement he needed. He spent the next few weeks getting to know his students. He talked with them about sports and family and holidays, finding out all sorts of interesting things about them and their lives along the way.

Finally the day came to bring up another topic. "This week we're going to talk about God," Dave announced at the beginning of class.

He asked one of his students, "Do you believe in God?"

"No, I don't," said the young man.

"Why not?" Dave asked.

"Well, nobody believes in God."

He went to the next person. "What about you?"

"I'm an atheist," she answered.

"Why are you an atheist?" Dave asked.

"I don't know, my parents are atheists, all my friends are atheists."

Around the room he went, hearing from each student, with many saying essentially the same thing: "Everybody knows he doesn't exist."

Except for one student, Mirka, who'd been a believer for six months, no one believed in God. But they didn't know *why* they didn't believe. Many of them had not rejected Jesus; they just

hadn't learned about him yet. They didn't have enough information about him to make a decision. They didn't understand God's love, or the sacrifice he'd made for them.

So the next day Dave said, "I believe in God and let me tell you why."

He drew the bridge illustration on the board, showing man on one side and God on the other, and explained the problem of sin that separated the two. He then went on to share about Jesus, how he came to earth, lived a perfect life, died for our sins and was then raised to life, thus making a bridge between God and us. He finished by telling how Jesus made a difference in his own life.

When he finished and class was dismissed, he looked up at the board and thought, *Is this legal?*

That began a series of conversations with the students. It was so much fun for Dave to share Christ and talk about spiritual things with them.

In May he asked the students, "What are you doing this summer?"

"Nothing," they answered.

"What do you mean nothing; won't you get a job?" he asked.

"No, it's hard to get a job."

"Well, what about family vacation?" Dave persisted.

"Yeah, maybe we'll go for a week, but both my parents work so they're not at home much. I'll just be sitting at home all summer."

Another student said, "You know, before Communism fell, we all went to camp for two or three weeks. But now that Young Pioneers [the Communist youth organization] doesn't have camp anymore, we don't have anything to do."

The student continued, "If you would do a camp for us, and teach English at it, our parents would let us go. And you could even talk about God if you wanted! As long as you do it all in English, they'll send us."

This got Dave's heart beating! *An English camp, where we could talk about God*, Dave thought, *that would be an incredible opportunity.*

He began to dream and take steps to make it a reality.

Needing native English speakers, Dave called his brother, who was in Heidelberg leading a Malachi youth group. "Hey, Josh, do you think you could get enough of your students together for a mission trip and come do an English camp with us this summer?" he asked. Josh said he'd see what he could do.

Several days later Dave came to the students saying, "I liked your idea about an English camp. I'm working on putting one together for you. How many of you would like to come to a camp with me?"

After a show of many hands, Dave started planning.

Dave had been planning camps and retreats in Germany for years. Finding a location, planning activities, training staff and inviting students had never been a problem. But now we were in a completely new location, learning the language and still building relationships with these kids. Dave wondered if it would work.

By this time we'd learned that I was pregnant with baby number three, due in late October. I was in the high-risk category because of my history, so my Czech doctor recommended I do nothing more than light work at home and care for our two boys.

Much easier said than done.

A friend offered to come from the States to help me for the summer while Dave planned and prepared for camp. Karen Brewster was invaluable, playing with the boys and helping me around the house, all during the hottest summer in over fifty years.

One evening we were in the living room eating dinner. Caleb, one and a half by now, was already bathed and ready for bed. Running around in his footie pajamas, he went from squealing in delight to screaming in anguish, all within just seconds.

This was not out of the ordinary with Caleb. Whereas Tyler had been our cautious one, Caleb was the daredevil. He seemed fearless, and was always on the move. So we didn't take the piercing screams too seriously.

"Come here, Caleb, let me see what happened," I said as I picked him up.

Because he wasn't speaking many words yet, he couldn't tell us what had happened. While he cried, I looked him over for blood or bruises, and not finding any, assumed he merely bumped into something. I thought that kisses and cuddles from Mommy would take care of it.

But the crying didn't stop. He continued to alternately wail and whimper for over an hour.

"Karen, I think you'd better go find Dave. I don't know what's wrong, but it doesn't feel normal," I said as I held him on my lap while he whimpered.

At Karen's request, Dave came inside and began to look Caleb over more carefully.

"Do you think we should take him to the hospital?" I asked.

"Let's wait a little bit longer and see if he calms down. It will be quite an ordeal to go in there since we don't have Czech insurance yet. I don't know what they'll do with us if we just show up with our American insurance cards."

But Caleb continued to cry, so Dave called Vladek and asked him to meet us at the hospital.

Once there, with doctors, nurses and other personnel beside us, we felt like we were in good hands, though the equipment and decor looked like we were back in the 1950s.

They didn't let us go with him for an X-ray, but we heard his screams down the hall. It was difficult to sit and wait.

They returned him to us, and we waited for what seemed like hours to hear the results. The doctor finally came in with his news.

"Your son has a clean break on his right femur. He will need to be admitted to the hospital. We'll put him in a cast and keep him here for observation."

Dave tried to ask if hospitalization was necessary, but there was no budging. Caleb was going to be admitted.

"Well, then, I'd like to stay with him," Dave declared.

"That's not possible. We don't allow that," the doctor said through translation.

"But my son is just eighteen months old, doesn't understand Czech and I don't want him to be alone," Dave persisted.

"Well, this is out of the ordinary, but I'll see what I can do," the doctor said, finishing the conversation.

Dave whispered to me that we'd better prepare ourselves emotionally for the fact that they might not let him stay. He also assured me he would do everything he could to make it happen.

Nurses came in and took Caleb from us again, and we heard his cries all the way down the hallway. There was nothing for us to do but wait.

Eventually, they called for us and led us to where Caleb was already in bed. His leg was held up in the air by pulleys, levers and old leather weights. I started to cry. His cast ran from his toes all the way up around his waist, leaving just a little hole where a diaper lay under him.

"What have they done to him?" I cried out. I'm not sure who was crying more, Caleb or me.

A nurse came in and said they'd found a place for Dave to spend the night. While he wasn't allowed in the room with Caleb, he could stay there until he fell asleep, and then go to his room: a storage closet with a cot inside.

I left in our car, alone, to drive home, crying as I went. Our first camp was to start in just two weeks. How would we manage all the necessary preparations for it with Caleb in the hospital? On top of this, I was feeling small contractions and knew I needed to be careful for the sake of the baby inside me.

"Oh, Lord, help us," I prayed silently as I drove home.

God's Promise
Call on me when you are in trouble and I will rescue you.
Psalm 91:15

CHAPTER TWENTY

Stuck in Germany

A fter four days, they released Caleb to our care and we brought him home.

The plaster cast weighed at least ten pounds, which made carrying him quite difficult. We moved him from his crib to the couch at the beginning of a day, and back at the end. His days were awfully long, as he lay there unable to move. We tried to make sure someone was near him most of the day since he was so uncomfortable and needed distraction.

In the meantime, Dave worked feverishly to prepare for the upcoming camp. Since there were only four in our church's youth group, we "borrowed" Christians from other churches to be at the camp, along with the group of Americans from the military base in Heidelberg who would come to teach and speak in English.

One day we received a static-filled phone call from a young American man in Romania. Somehow he'd heard of what we were doing in Czech and asked if he could come to see us.

Dave asked in reply, "How soon could you get here? We've got an English camp in just a few days and could sure use some more help."

Todd Morr arrived by train days later and joined Dave at the first JV English camp held in the Beskydy Mountains, with eighty people packed into an old hotel to share a week of life together.

I was only able to visit the camp once because Caleb was still in his cast. With the help of a friend visiting from Germany that week, we made a trip one afternoon to see what was going on.

I couldn't believe my eyes! The level of excitement, participation and community was clearly evident. Everyone was having a great time, but most importantly, the non-Christian students were open and interested in hearing more about God.

After every evening program, during discussion groups, they asked difficult and penetrating questions, trying to make sense of what they were hearing. For most of them, it was the first time they'd heard about Jesus and what it means to have faith in him.

By the end of the week, many were open to continuing to learn more about all they'd heard. While no one made a profession of faith that week, we felt a barrier had been breached and that the doors were now open into their hearts and lives.

Dave announced to them that there would be a follow-up party once school started in September, and that they were all

invited to our house for it. We hoped that many of them would come.

After the week of camp, Dave and Todd talked about his future, and it was decided that he would stay for a few months to follow up on relationships with students who had been at camp. He moved into a spare room on the bottom floor of our house and began reaching out to students, playing basketball, meeting at cafés and inviting them over to hang out.

Shortly after camp, we received some difficult news. Rich Kerns, the pastor at Grace Church of DuPage, who had reached out to us, mentored Dave during our year there and gone to bat for us to be Grace Church missionaries, was in his last days on earth. Having battled brain cancer for several years, Rich knew his days were limited, so sent word to Dave to come see him one last time.

Dave spent a precious week back in the Chicago area with Rich, sitting with him and talking about the Lord, life and what was next for both of them. Rich's wife, Theresa, and their three children were nearby each day as their husband and dad slipped toward heaven. He gave of himself to many in his final days.

Dave filled a notebook with Rich's words of wisdom, insight and instructions as he spoke into Dave's life with one foot on earth and one in heaven. When Dave left, he knew he wouldn't see his friend and mentor again in this life.

Dave returned with a heavy heart, and we began to think toward our trip to northern Germany where we would be attending a conference with our mission organization. Karen had gone home by then, so I was managing the boys on my own, with Caleb still in his cast. Pregnant and trying to prepare to be

away for a week, I was glad to have Dave home, though grateful he'd been able to be with Rich and his family that week.

Able to help me with Caleb again, the next morning Dave held him over the bathtub (to keep the leg from getting wet), and I used the showerhead to give him a bath. As Dave shifted him so I could better reach his head, his cries pierced the air.

Upon examination, we found that the cast had worn a hole into his skin just below the edge of the cast on his waistline. We whisked Caleb into the car and off to the hospital, as we knew the cast would have to come off in order to treat it.

The hole was not just infected. Once the doctor cut off the cast and looked at it, he could see it had rubbed all the way through to the bone of his spine, creating a half-dollar-size hole on his back. The doctors began the difficult process of debriding, removing the damaged and infected skin from the area. We were in outpatient care every day for the next week.

The doctor put a new cast on his leg, leaving room at the waistline so the hole could be reached for treatment. While this made it easier on the doctor, it meant that Caleb could no longer lie comfortably on his back, only on his side. His (and my) days were excruciatingly long until the day arrived to remove the cast. Caleb had his cast taken off on my thirty-third birthday. It was the best birthday present I had ever received.

The next day we set off in our van for the conference in Germany.

Four-year-old Tyler was ecstatic at the prospect of being out of the house and on to something more interesting. After spending many days playing beside Caleb on the couch, he was glad to be in his car seat, looking out the window, playing with

toys in his lap. On the other hand, Caleb was not so happy to be strapped into a car seat. He desperately wanted to scoot around and be mobile. It was a long ten-hour drive.

Seven months pregnant, I was exhausted. After the hottest summer on record, and all that had occurred, I was ready for a break. Although it was a long trip to get there, I was looking forward to the time of teaching, worship and fellowship, with good child care for the boys during part of the day.

The next four days at the conference were a sweet relief. I enjoyed time with new and old friends and felt refreshed by the worship and teaching.

On the last afternoon of the conference, I wasn't feeling well. I opted out of a session and went back to our room while the boys were still in child care. I hoped I could get some rest and feel better for the evening program. But by dinnertime, I felt faint and flushed. I was afraid I was coming down with the flu.

On top of that, we received word from the States that Rich, our pastor, had passed away that morning. I grieved as I lay in bed, wrestling with the joy of his being out of his suffering and with the Lord, yet knowing the pain that this left his wife and three children with. It was a sad evening for me.

Dave had tucked the boys into bed and gone to the evening program while I stayed in our room. By 8:30, I was feeling worse. But this time, I knew it was more than the flu.

Contractions were coming every ten minutes.

With no way to get up, and no possibility to contact Dave in the meeting, I lay in bed praying, willing him to arrive back to the room to help me.

Thankfully, Laura stopped by to check on me, and I alerted her to the situation. She rushed to find Dave. When he got to the room, it was apparent I needed to get to a hospital.

After asking the front desk of the hotel for the nearest one, Dave and I rushed out into the summer night air, while Laura stayed behind with the sleeping boys.

At only thirty-two weeks, I had no idea if I was about to deliver our daughter.

As I lay in the emergency room, hooked up to monitors and an IV, thoughts swirled through my head. *What are we going to do if I deliver tonight? Is she okay? Will there be complications? What if we have to stay here because she's not okay?* I couldn't stop my worried thoughts.

Dave stood by my side, alternating between praying and comforting me. We waited anxiously for the doctor's news.

"Frau Patty," the German doctor began as soon as he arrived. "You are dilated, but we've been able to slow the contractions down to prevent delivery for now. However, you'll need to stay here in the hospital for the duration of your pregnancy."

Tears sprang to my eyes. I knew exactly what he'd said, even though he'd spoken German.

"Dave?" I whimpered.

Dave asked if he could talk with the doctor in the hall, so they slipped out of the room while I lay in bed beginning to panic.

When Dave came back in, it was with a great deal of compassion, but weariness, in his eyes. "We have to trust the Lord with this, Connie. This isn't a mistake," he began. "The doctor says that there are no signs of problems with the baby, so that's

good news. But it's too soon for her to come, and if you were to travel, it would induce labor. They are not willing to let you go because of that danger, and I think they're right."

"So what do we do?" I asked in disbelief.

We were in northern Germany, knew no one there and the conference was ending in the morning, so Dave and the boys had nowhere to go. I looked at the prospect of spending up to two months in a hospital I didn't know and felt overwhelmed. "God, where are you?" I cried out.

Dave responded gently, "Let me work on some things. You know I'll figure this out. The most important thing is that our daughter arrives safely. We're not going to put her, or you, in jeopardy. So relax, try to rest, and I'll be back in the morning."

It was a very long night as I lay in the hospital bed.

I felt disbelief more than fear at that point. I wanted to trust the Lord, but I was also confused about why he was allowing this to happen. Everything in me wanted to make sense of it, but nothing did as I wrestled with him throughout the night.

Dave didn't arrive until just before noon the next day. With no way to reach him, no books or magazines to look at and no one else in my room to talk to, it was a long wait. He was a sight for sore eyes when he walked into the room. After checking in to see how I was doing, and assurances from him that the boys were fine, he gave me his thoughts.

"The doctor says you're still having contractions, so it's imperative that you lie still and let yourself be taken care of by them. That's the most important thing right now! I've checked the boys and me out of the hotel, and Laura is with them right now. I don't have much time, because she and Dan need to get

on the road and head back to Poland. This means I won't get to visit you, because the boys are not allowed up here. I'll check in with the doctors by phone several times a day, but you're going to have to brave this alone with the Lord for right now until I can figure out something else."

As I started to cry, he added, "I know this is very, very difficult for you. I'm really sorry you have to go through it. But it won't last forever, and we WILL get through it. Trust the Lord, Connie. He's here with you, and he won't leave you." After a few more words of love and assurance, he left the room. I didn't know when I would see him again.

I was thankful that the doctors and nurses were kind and understanding, so it wasn't an unpleasant experience in that way. But it was definitely a long day and night again, praying, crying out to the Lord for his help.

Another full day passed with only seeing Dave for a few minutes. Neither he nor I remember whom he left the boys with while he rushed up to my room to say hello and give me words of encouragement and support.

The next morning, Dave entered my room, this time with the boys in tow. "I'm checking you out," he said as he began to put my things in a bag.

Still hugging the boys, I asked incredulously, "How?"

"I'll tell you about it when we get to the van," he replied.

Nurses came in with papers to sign, and brought a wheelchair to take me out in. Before I knew it, I was lying in the back of our van. We sat in the hospital's parking lot as Dave explained the events of the past two days. "The boys and I have had a great time, haven't we?" he said, turning to them.

Tyler was enthusiastic as he responded, "Mommy, we fed the ducks in the park for a long time! And we spent two nights sleeping in the van!"

"You did what?" I turned to Dave, shocked.

"Well, yes ... we did. I decided to just turn it into an adventure with the boys. Plus, it saved money. Good thing they had their blankets—I think they slept fine. It was a little cold for me without one ..." he said with a smile on his face.

"I've been making some phone calls and it all started to come together yesterday afternoon. But then I had to talk with the doctor here to make sure you were really okay to make this plan work. He actually wouldn't release you himself, so I had to take personal responsibility for you and sign a waiver saying that if anything happened, they weren't liable."

"You did what?" I asked again. "How much danger am I in? And where are we going?"

"He said you and the baby are stable, but that you need to be on strict bed rest for the next four weeks. He would prefer you did that in the hospital. But I knew that wasn't going to work for any of us. So I've made other plans."

I was anxious to hear what those plans were.

"We're going to drive down to Heidelberg, and you're going to stay at my brother's house in Heidelberg for a month while I drive back to Havířov with the boys so I can be there in time for the reunion party with the kids from camp. Josh and Kristi are more than willing to help us out."

I stared at Dave, barely able to process that I would be staying with his brother and sister-in-law for a month.

"I'll stay at home with the boys while you rest and see Dr. Stork for checkups, and when she says that it's time to take you off bed rest and medication, then we'll come back. What do you think?"

I was silent. This meant I'd be having our baby girl in Germany. And that there was a chance, again, that Dave might not be there for the birth. "There isn't any way you can stay with me here in Germany?" I quietly pleaded.

"I know. I wish there were, I really do. But we've got people back home who can help me with the boys, and if we were here, I don't know where we'd live or what we'd do—Josh and Kristi don't have room for all of us.

"Plus, I feel like I've got to get back and help Todd and the others with the start of what we hope is a new beginning for our youth group. This is such a crucial time to be there for that. You've got to rest and not be under any stress. If we're here, that will be hard to do."

With the happy chatter of the boys in their car seats, and Dave's heart in his hand, offering me the best solution he could come up with, I sighed and said, "Okay, if that's what we need to do, I'm willing."

We headed out onto the autobahn toward Heidelberg.

God's Promise
I am with you and I will help you because I am your God.
Isaiah 41:10

CHAPTER TWENTY-ONE *Good News, Bad News*

Against the doctor's wishes, we made one stop on our way to Heidelberg.

For months, a reunion had been planned among six of us women who were with Malachi near its beginnings in the early 1980s. Jerri, Joyce, Laura, Lori, Ruth and I were all to meet up for two days and nights together to catch up for the first time in years.

I was devastated to miss it, thinking I wouldn't be able to go because of everything that had happened. But knowing that I needed those friends more than ever, Dave made all the arrangements. I would stay in bed *and* get the girl time I needed. It was a huge gift to be with them, and I was deeply blessed by how they served and took care of me during those days.

Arriving at Josh and Kristi's home near Heidelberg a few days later, I felt bolstered and ready for what was ahead. Knowing that it was best not to prolong the goodbye, Dave and

the boys only stayed one night before getting on the road back to Czech.

Women we knew from our days of serving in the Heidelberg chapel loaded him down with groceries from the commissary, and sent him happily on his way with Kraft Macaroni and Cheese, Raisin Bran and Grape Nuts cereal, and other such American delicacies. I was so thankful for their kindness and generosity to my family.

But as they drove away, I sobbed. Lying on a mattress on the floor in my brother and sister-in-law's dining room (so I could see out the window, as well as be part of their lives when they were home), I grieved. Phone calls were still too expensive at that time for anything more than a quick check-in, there was no Internet to connect with and we didn't have cell phones so there was no texting. I knew contact with Dave and the boys would be limited, and that I would miss them all terribly.

However, in God's kindness, over the next few days he brought a sense of safety and protection by bringing me back to the Heidelberg area. I could rest, being back to familiarity: care from the doctor who knew me, friends who lavished love and food on me and family who kept me company. It turned out to be a relief to be there.

Four weeks went by as I lay day after day in the dining room. I jokingly began to call it "My Other German Vacation," remembering our story from the time in the hospital with Tyler four years earlier.

Finally, on September 26, I reached thirty-six weeks. Dr. Stork gave me the okay to go off bed rest and medication. After many ultrasounds, she was confident that our baby girl would

be healthy even if she came early. She told me to contact Dave and tell him the birth was imminent.

My friend Jerri and her husband, Jay, had rented our apartment in St. Leon after we had moved to Czech a year earlier. In the Lord's providence, they were due to be in the States for a two-month home assignment, so offered to let us stay in our old home.

Dave arrived back with the boys, and we moved over to the house on Schulstrasse in St. Leon on the night of September 28. I expected to go into labor anytime.

But I didn't.

Day after day went by as we waited for our little girl's arrival.

In many ways it was a gift, since I needed the time to reconnect with Dave, as well as the boys, before having a new baby to focus on. We visited the zoo, went swimming, played at the park, shopped and visited friends and family. We fondly referred to it as "OUR German vacation" as the days passed by.

Finally, ten days after Dave and the boys had returned to Germany, I went into labor on the morning of October 8. After almost being born in August, and then September, she was an October baby after all! Claire Alyce made her debut later that afternoon. There were no complications, and she was healthy.

An infection kept me in the hospital longer than Claire needed to be there. She roomed with me until I was well, ten days later. German hospitals and I just couldn't seem to get enough of each other.

Finally able to come home with a third baby, it was a joy to be a family again, and a relief to be nearing our time to return home to Czech. We hoped to leave a few days later.

Dave made a trip to the embassy to pick up Claire's passport, while I braved it alone at the apartment with all three kids for the first time. When Dave didn't arrive back at the time I expected, I didn't know whether to be upset or worried. It had been a long day of trying to meet everyone's needs, and I was spent.

Finally, hours later, Dave walked in wearily. By the look on his face, I could see he hadn't been gone purposely.

"I've got some good news and some bad news," he said with a sigh.

"Well, you'd better tell the good news first so I'm ready for what's next," I said with my own sigh, as I sat on the couch holding Claire in one arm and Caleb in the other.

"I picked up Claire's passport with no problem."

"And the bad news?" I asked, with no clue of what he was going to say.

"The engine blew on our van. It's gone. I had to get someone to tow me from near Darmstadt all the way to Herr Just's garage in Kirrlach."

I sat in stunned silence.

Finally, I asked, "Well, what's next?"

"First of all, I felt really bad that I couldn't call you and let you know what was happening. I had to trust that the Lord would take care of you and the kids while you were waiting. Sorry I'm so late."

"Are you kidding? That's totally okay!" I honestly answered.

He continued, "Herr Just says it'll be about four thousand dollars to replace the engine."

Really? I thought. *This is happening right now, after we've just brought our daughter home from the hospital?*

Before I could even say anything, Dave added, "And the Lord spoke to me right out of his Word as I was being towed and said, 'Dave, you've got to give me thanks for this. Don't forget to rejoice either.' You know how I was just reading Thessalonians? Well, now's the time to put that into practice."

So right there we told the Lord we were thankful and chose to rejoice. With no funds in our account, we knew our only hope was the Lord's supernatural provision. We sat down for dinner, and had a nice evening with the kids after that. What else was there to do?

The next day, while Herr Just searched for a used engine, Dave made a phone call to Grace Church in Chicago. They'd always told us that they wanted to know our needs and be alerted to pray any time we wanted to ask. This was as good of a time as any to take them up on their offer.

Dave explained the situation, asked for prayer and hung up, with assurances that they would indeed pray, and that they were concerned about us.

We continued to ask God to show us what to do. News came from Herr Just the next morning that he'd found an engine for the van, and he asked if we wanted him to put it in. Dave had to tell him we didn't have the money for it.

As I made lunch that day, nursed Claire and played with the boys in the afternoon, my heart cried out to the Lord for an answer. I just wanted to go home, but we had no way to get there.

That afternoon, the phone rang in the apartment. It was one of the elders from Grace Church. "Dave, we've been able to free up funds for you to fix your van! Tell us how much it is and we'll get it to you as soon as possible."

There was much rejoicing between Dave and me as he called the mechanic with the news. What an amazing provision from the Lord through our family at Grace Church. I felt so cared for by them and by him. Within two days the van was fixed, and we were on our way home.

It was good to see my house after being away for over two months. But I wasn't there for long. Leaving Dave at home with the boys, I raced over to Cieszyn, Poland, with baby Claire in her infant seat, to see Laura Hash, who we'd just learned was in the hospital, in labor.

Having not seen her since that night when she'd found me in my room at the hotel in Germany, in labor, it was a sweet reunion, especially since all was now well in my situation, and she was about to have her baby.

The next day she happily delivered their son, Jacob.

It was a delight to drive back over the next day to see him, albeit through glass, as the Polish hospital didn't allow visitors to see the baby in person. But I was glad to know that all was well with them too, and I was ready for us to get back to something like normal life.

With a new couple having joined our team by then, Josiah Venture now numbered nine adults and six children, and we'd lived in our two countries, Czech and Poland, just a few days short of one year. Not only were we growing in number, but through these trials, our faith was increasing as well. While it had been a difficult season for our family, it felt good to settle into normal routines with everyone healthy.

Dave had been right. Trusting in the Lord to see us through had absolutely been the right choice. There were so many ways

he had cared for us, been near to us and provided far beyond our imaginations.

That season of life was yet another test of my faith and willingness to say yes to the Lord and believe his promises. I chose to continue to follow him and trust him even when I couldn't see the way or understand the situation. I struggled through that time, but he sustained me. He spoke to me through his Word and through people time and time again, assuring me of his love, presence and plan for our lives.

It wasn't easy to trust, but I kept making conscious choices to do so. I felt my roots of faith deepening and wanted to continue strongly on that path of faith, no matter what else came our way.

God's Promise
I will not let you be tested beyond what you can endure.
1 Corinthians 10:13

CHAPTER TWENTY-TWO

Bursting at the Seams

While I'd been on bed rest in Germany, the camp reunion had far exceeded our expectations. More than sixty students showed up at our house in Havířov that first night. Dave and Todd moved all the furniture out of the living room, except for our piano and a china cabinet.

Students, as well as our little boys, packed in there for songs, games and a talk that continued down the path of what they'd heard at camp earlier in the summer.

We began to hold the youth group at our house every week, and kids began stopping by and hanging out. Dave and Todd had so many spiritual conversations with those students. They continued to walk them through Scripture and tell them real-life stories about what it looks like to know and follow God.

It seemed that a youth group filled a place in their lives, even though most were not believers yet. But they soaked in

our love, and plans were made to have another camp the following summer.

In the midst of those exciting days of growth, we realized our house was too small. Even with two floors, Dave could see that we needed more space to expand the ministry. Because there was still not much building in those days, it was difficult to find someone to take on the project of adding another floor to our house. But eventually we hired a firm, and they were there daily, building throughout the fall and into the winter.

There may have been firms who did better work at the time, but we didn't find them. Careless mistakes were made, such as hot and cold water plumbed backward, and hot water plumbed into the toilet. Dave also used an ax to chip up a whole layer of cement that was wrongly poured in our living room. The workers wouldn't do it.

Hoping to avoid anything worse than that, Dave climbed the ladder every day, up to the third floor, before stairs were put in, to oversee the construction, hoping nothing would go wrong.

One morning we woke up to quiet.

This was unusual on a weekday; the workmen were usually there by 6:30, jackhammering, pounding nails or using the electric saw. We all became early birds in those days.

After looking out the window and seeing no sign of the usual trucks in our driveway, Dave climbed upstairs to have a look around. Tools were laid here and there, and work clothes were on the ground, left where men had dropped them and changed into their own. Scaffolding covered the house, measuring tapes lay on ledges, and the cement mixer, which usually ran all day long, was silent.

"Maybe it's a holiday, or some kind of day off for the company. I guess they'll be back tomorrow," he said to me.

But they weren't. They never came back.

The tools stayed where they were, the scaffolding hung in its place and the cement mixer remained. Whether it was from poor business management, debts or other clients who hadn't paid, they went bankrupt and never returned to our house. We held on to the tools, clothing, scaffolding and cement mixer for years, thinking someday someone would come back for them. They never did.

It took months to find another firm willing to jump into our messy project. It's not really the job anyone wants to take. But thankfully, we tracked down a firm who began work in late spring and finished just before our September youth group kickoff. Claire took her first solid steps upstairs in the newly completed space the day before kids arrived.

After another successful English camp in August, students filled our house as they continued to be interested in spiritual things. Some put their faith in Christ over the next few months and came faithfully for Bible studies to learn more.

We found that students weren't as likely to make a decision at camp as they were after they'd been around us, come to youth group, read the Bible and had a chance to weigh for themselves the claims of Christ. Decisions were much more firm and rooted in true faith when they'd had time to contemplate the cost of following Jesus.

Most came from family backgrounds that didn't support their interest in spiritual things. It was an uphill battle for many as they pursued God against the wishes of their family. This was

always a difficulty as we worked with students: helping them to respect their parents while at the same time respond to the Word of God and promptings of the Spirit.

There were some who made professions of faith, but then were forbidden from attending youth group or going to church. We told these students to respect their parents, though some came secretly, hungry to know more.

We were thrilled about what was starting to take place in young people's lives as we began to see the fulfillment of the vision God had given Dave. But that doesn't mean we still didn't feel like fish out of water, living in a country where we were out of place and seen as foreigners.

While Dave spoke fluent Czech within two years, I struggled to catch up, busy with three small children at home. I tried to speak Czech as often as I could when I was out at the grocery store, post office, at church or the doctor's office.

I made funny mistakes, like all new missionaries do. I accidentally told the woman at the grocery store that I was German. When I asked for eggs, I was sent to the restroom. At church the older gentleman who asked me how I was each week suddenly changed the question and left me tongue-tied when I no longer had an answer. I avoided him for weeks after that.

During those long months of pregnancy, Laura and I talked by way of a special radiophone our husbands had rigged up. Radio antennas on top of our houses allowed us to spend hours discussing the ins and outs of pregnancies and how we were coping with life in Czech and in Poland. Each night we had a standing 10 p.m. call scheduled if either of us needed to talk.

After months of these conversations, our Czech neighbor came over one evening with a request. "Tonight, there is big hockey at ten. Can you ask wife to make call at different time so I watch?" he asked in broken English.

We found out that the radio signal of our phones disrupted his television service every time we used them! His picture became a fuzzy blur, and he tuned into our conversation clear as could be, on his television. Depending on how well they understood our English, when we made our nightly calls, he and his family heard all sorts of information about pregnancy, what we'd found in the store that day and how we were feeling about life in our respective countries.

We also found out that we shared a telephone line with them. We had no idea. Then, an entire year later, we found out we shared a telephone line with still another neighbor! A young woman stopped by our house one afternoon and sweetly asked if it was okay if we could please make the line available at 7 that night so they could make an important call.

I grew up on a party line in my Oregon childhood days, and knew the sound of a receiver being picked up or put down, but I never heard that on our phone in Havířov. Who knows what else our neighbors heard in those days.

God's Promise
I have chosen the weak things of this world to confound
the strong.
1 Corinthians 1:27

CHAPTER TWENTY-THREE *Dreams and Visions*

I n the winter of 1995, we had two visitors come from the
States.

Dann Spader was a longtime friend and mentor to
Dave. He started Sonlife Ministries years earlier out of Moody
Bible Institute, and we were beginning to use his materials to
train youth leaders in Czech and Poland. He and Dave Garda,
his partner in the ministry, came out to see what God was doing, and to be an encouragement to us.

As Dave drove them around the area, they passed an old
recreational facility that had been used as a camp for Young
Pioneers, the Communist youth program. "You ought to buy
a place like that," Dann said. "You could probably get it for a
song and wouldn't have to do much with it. Just use it 'as is' for
a youth camp, or bring your leaders in for training. It'd be great
if you had a place of your own like that."

The idea burrowed into Dave's mind, and he began to dream about buying a small camp facility over the next months. In the spring and summer, he drove to every recreational facility within an hour's drive. There were hundreds of them, built by companies under Communism. Some were youth camps; others were hotels for the employees of companies such as the coal mines in Ostrava.

Dave decided to personally visit one hundred twenty of them. He wasn't just looking at the ones that were for sale. He wanted to see the range of possibility to find which facilities were the best.

By fall, he had his favorites and was anxious to show them to me. One afternoon we drove up to the mountains, passing through Frýdek-Místek, and on to Frýdlant and Ostravicí. From there we headed toward Lysá hora, the highest mountain in the range. After pulling up to a rundown building that looked like an old hotel, Dave stopped the car.

"Of all the places that I've been to over these past months, this is my number one choice. What do you think?" Dave asked.

"Wow! It's spectacular! I love it up here," I answered. "Is it for sale?"

"I don't think so," Dave said. "I tried to talk with someone, but didn't get an answer. Wouldn't this make a great location for a camp, though?" he asked enthusiastically.

I agreed. I was mesmerized by the view at Hotel Malenovice, and even though the building was nothing special, there was a charm about the area that overcame its deficiencies. "Do you have any idea how much places are going for? I mean, the ones that *are* for sale?" I asked.

"It's actually not as cheap as you'd think. In dollars, it's maybe 100,000 to 200,000. And I don't know what you get for that, if it's just the building, or what's inside too. I haven't gotten that far yet … I'm just dreaming and thinking about how great it would be to have a Josiah Venture camp—kind of a home for the movement. We could bring kids here and do camps; we could have leaders up for retreats and trainings. We could even do our staff retreats here, though we'd kind of ramble around in such a big building," he said with a laugh.

Standing out on the terrace of the hotel, overlooking the valley, Dave prayed while Tyler and Caleb ran around and I held Claire in my arms. It was a bold prayer to ask for this place.

It seemed like an overwhelming project to me, but I could imagine how great it would be to have a place of our own. After having just finished two camps at rented facilities, I could see how it would be a great advantage to own a place. We could staff it with Christians and create our own atmosphere, choose our own food, make as much noise as we wanted and do our own programs with no restrictions.

Driving away, I felt prompted to begin praying diligently for this very place. We talked about it a lot in the following weeks. Was this really something the Lord was calling us to believe him for? Did we have enough faith to do something like this? The most we'd ever raised for anything up until then was $8,000 for our red VW van. How on earth would God raise up $100,000 to buy an old Communist hotel?

We made inquiries, and found that the hotel, simply called Hotel Malenovice, had been built on land taken from the village of Malenovice under Communism. With the change to

a democratic system, properties were being returned to their rightful owners, and Hotel Malenovice had been restituted to the village a few years earlier.

But the town's leadership had plans for it. They had applied to the European Union for a grant to turn it into a home for the elderly. They made it clear they were not interested in selling.

So Dave began to look elsewhere.

Across the valley, on the side of a 2,900-foot mountain in the Beskydys, was a building that *was* for sale. Hotel Ondřejník, a sixty-bed hotel and favorite destination of hikers in the region, was Dave's second choice in the area. Alongside it was Solárka, an old wooden hotel with a similar capacity that had been repossessed by the bank and would eventually be for sale too. These also had amazing views of the valley and would allow us to have room for growth. Dave began to pursue purchasing these two buildings instead.

In the spring of 1996, our friend Karen, who had helped us the summer I was pregnant with Claire, came back to stay for a month. Toward the end of her time with us, Dave took her up to see the hotel that had first captured his heart. Even though it wasn't for sale, he wanted her to see it.

While standing on the same terrace we'd stood on months earlier dreaming and praying, Dave showed her the view across the valley to the other two hotels, sharing his vision to purchase them. Even though we were standing in front of Hotel Malenovice, the place that was his first choice, he knew that it wasn't a possibility and that we needed to move forward on the other ones.

As we looked over the valley, Karen said, "I'm going to tell my parents about this place, and they'll pray too. I hope they'll get to visit someday and see what God does."

Just a few months later, a gift of $10,000 arrived. "This is seed money for those hotels that you want to purchase for the youth there. We pray God multiplies it a hundredfold and makes a way for you to purchase the place of his choosing." The note was signed by Jim and Barbara, her parents.

Not long afterward, another gift arrived for the same amount. Dave hadn't even started fund-raising, yet God was moving in the hearts of his people. We were beside ourselves with joy at the thought that God was making his plan clear.

In the fall of 1996, Dave began to share the vision for a Josiah Venture training facility. He and Jim Miller, one of our new teammates, put together a beautiful book of photos and information about the vision. Dave made numerous trips to the States, speaking in churches, talking with individuals and sharing with foundations about God's movement among the youth in Eastern Europe, and how we envisioned a home for them in these two side-by-side hotels.

Over the next year, through the generosity of many, $240,000 was given. By the fall of 1997, we were ready to make the purchase.

But it didn't happen. While Hotel Ondřejník was still for sale, Solárka was tied up in a legal battle.

Month after month, our lawyer pursued every avenue, but the property remained locked up in the bank system. We heard that some sort of Mafia was involved, and even that our lawyer's life had been threatened. Doberman pinschers stood guard at the hotel,

and we were never able to go inside to look at it. The owner of Ondřejník was anxious to sell, but without the ability to purchase Solárka, we couldn't proceed. There wasn't enough room in just one hotel for what we envisioned. We really needed both places.

So we waited.

Months passed with no word. People who'd been praying for the project were writing to ask if we'd purchased the buildings yet. Donors wanted to know what had happened. The committee in the States who helped Dave with fund-raising was anxious for a conclusion to their efforts.

It was a difficult time for all of us. God had led us so far, and now we seemed to be at the end of a canyon, with no way out.

One bright spot during those days was the registration in August 1997 of a nonprofit organization in the Czech Republic, the first European partner with Josiah Venture. KAM, an acronym for Křesťanská akademie mladých (Christian Academy of Youth), was a play on words in Czech. The word *kam* means "where" or implies "where are you going?" The answer: with God.

We were going with God, but that didn't mean we knew *where* we were going. God's road isn't always a straight path, and at that point we couldn't see the way ahead for our dream of a training center in the Czech Republic.

In the spring, Dave was feeling heavy about the whole situation.

Remembering how he had fasted and prayed for God's direction years earlier as we contemplated moving to Eastern Europe to begin the ministry, he decided to do the same once again. He said to the Lord, "I'm going to fast and pray until I hear from you."

In a hotel in the mountains, he began to fast on Monday, awaiting how God was going to answer.

On Tuesday, he had a great time in prayer, but no answer.

Wednesday came and nothing happened, except he was very hungry.

By Thursday, it was painful for him. And still, there was no answer.

On Friday, he tried to prepare for a training seminar he was supposed to teach that night. He was having a hard time concentrating to prepare for it. But as he prayed that morning, he finally sensed the Lord saying something to him.

"It's taken care of, you can break your fast."

"What's taken care of? Could you be more specific?" he asked the Lord.

But God said nothing more. Trusting he'd heard correctly, Dave broke his fast in faith that God had spoken, and finished his preparation for the training session.

That evening as he spoke, he shared the prayer request about our desire to purchase the two hotels. While speaking, he noticed a white-haired lady in the back, which was unusual, because the rest of the youth leaders attending were under the age of thirty.

After his talk, she came to him and said, "You mentioned you were praying for a hotel. Let me tell you something that happened to me. I used to work in these mountains in one of these hotels, and one day I was praying and I had a vision. I saw a hotel up on a mountain. It was big and beautiful, and people came from all over the world to see what God was doing there. From that place spread revival to the whole region."

Dave nearly dropped his cup of coffee. Squeezing the flimsy cup, with hot coffee brimming over onto his hand, he managed to ask, "You saw *what*?"

"I saw something like what you described. Yes, I've been praying for such a place as that," she said.

"Well, keep praying!" Dave exclaimed.

She said, "I don't need to keep praying, it's already prayed up." And she walked away.

Reeling from this interchange, Dave thought, *What just happened?* Soon he gathered himself and went to find her. "Excuse me, but could I just ask: Who are you and how did you get here? Do you work with young people?"

"No, I don't," she answered.

"Well, how did you get here?" Dave asked, perplexed.

"Oh, it was kind of by accident. I was in the Ostrava church praying today. I don't actually go there—I go to the apostolic church in Opava. But I was in the Ostrava church and when I finished, I saw a group of young people in the foyer, and I asked, 'Where are you going?' and they said, 'We're going to a seminar on praise and worship.' I then asked, 'Can I go?' They told me it was actually overnight, but then I asked, 'Well, does anyone have an extra toothbrush? I'll go! I can just sleep in my clothes.' So that's how I got here."

With that she left Dave and went to mingle with some of the young people. Dave didn't know what to think. She'd been at a church she didn't usually go to, gotten in the car with people she didn't know and come to a training seminar for youth leaders when she wasn't one. And she'd had a vision. Shaking his head, he wondered what that was all about.

Two days later, Dave met with the pastor of the church in Ostrava where she said she'd been praying. "I had the strangest thing happen this weekend," he said to the pastor. "I met a white-haired lady at the training seminar your youth leaders were at. She said she sometimes comes to your church to pray. Do you know her?"

The pastor thought for a moment, and then answered, "No, I don't think so."

"Well, she said she doesn't actually go to your church. She goes to the apostolic church in Opava."

The pastor looked bewildered. "That's strange. There is no apostolic church in Opava."

And it's true. There isn't.

Dave never saw the white-haired woman again. But it made him wonder. Had she been a real person, or a messenger sent from God? He knew that Hebrews 13:2 says, "Some people have entertained angels without knowing it." Was she one of those?

In either case, it was a miraculous answer to his prayer of "God, are we on the right track?"

Her vision gave us courage to believe we were.

"I saw a hotel up on a mountain. It was big and beautiful, and people came from all over the world to see what God was doing there. From that place spread revival to the whole region."

God's Promise
If you wait for me I will work on your behalf.
Isaiah. 64:4

CHAPTER TWENTY-FOUR

It Is Unanimous

I n June, Hotel Solárka was finally available for purchase.

There was a lot of rejoicing among our team. God had finally unlocked the door and we were going to walk, literally and figuratively, through the doorway.

We made arrangements to go inside Solárka for the first time. A specialist from Prague came with us to inspect the building's structural soundness. The anticipation of finally being able to see the building was palpable as we stood outside. We'd been waiting for it with prayer and anguish for a year and a half.

But I was carrying a concern that day, one I hadn't yet shared with Dave since we'd been busy with camp that morning. (We were running our first English camp for parents, across the valley at Hotel Malenovice.)

When our daughter, Claire, just a few months short of three years old, had come down to breakfast that morning, something appeared to be wrong with her eyes. Two friends who

were there from the States for camp noticed first, since I was sitting next to her at the table. Theresa whispered, "Connie, have you noticed anything strange about Claire's eyes today?"

I asked Claire a question so she would look at me. Her eyes were completely crossed. Wondering if it was because she was still tired, I tried to shake off my concerns and not make too much of it. But later in the morning, I saw the same thing: distinct crossing of her eyes. I couldn't imagine what had happened.

Trying not to worry about it as we stood in front of the beautiful wooden hotel, I prayed for wisdom to know what to do if it continued. As I stepped into the building with everyone else, I prayed that it wouldn't.

While the specialist poked around the old wooden hotel, Dave and the rest of us admired the quaintness of the building and the magnificence of the view as we dreamed about what could happen here.

The building was a mess inside. It hadn't been used for years, so would require renovation to restore it to its former glory. But we were up for the task! We'd waited so long for it that we didn't mind the thought of all the work ahead of us.

Standing out on the lawn afterward in the warm sunshine, we soaked in the faithfulness of God that had led us this far. It had been a long wait, but now we were on the verge of signing the contract and beginning to prepare it for young people.

"Dave, I'd like to talk over my findings," the specialist said as we walked toward our cars. "Is there a place we could meet?" he asked.

"How about over there?" Dave asked, pointing to show where we were staying that week. "We're across the valley at

Hotel Malenovice doing a camp. Why don't you follow us over there and we can meet in the dining room," Dave said.

Several hours later, Dave found me. "You are not going to believe what happened this afternoon. I sat down with the specialist when we got back and his first words to me were, 'If I were you, I wouldn't buy that building.'"

"What? Why did he say that?" I asked, stunned to hear this news.

"The building has sat for too long and has extensive water damage in the foundation. Not only that, but the water supply is not adequate. He said we would have to figure out how to get more in there to support the amount of guests we're anticipating.

"He also said the building is not up to code for fire standards and would have to be completely renovated from the foundation up in order to pass inspections. He had a list several pages long of other things wrong with it."

His last words to Dave: "You'd be pouring money down a pit if you bought that building."

I sat speechless in front of him, unable to process this news. "What do we do now?" I asked in disbelief.

"Well, this is where it gets really interesting," Dave said with a grin. "As we were finishing up our conversation he said, 'You know, what you need is a building like this one,' waving his arm across the room where we sat. 'It's not beautiful, but it's on a solid foundation and would be a much better investment of your money. What it needs is cosmetic changes, not structural ones.'

"I told him that we'd tried to buy it several years ago," Dave said, "but that it wasn't for sale. His response was, 'That's really too bad, because it would be a much better building for you.'

"He then walked away, and I was sitting at the table reeling from his news," Dave said. "I felt like I'd been punched in the gut and was imagining how I would have to tell everyone that we didn't get it. I was also thinking about how hard it would be to start over, to begin the process of looking for another place."

He paused and looked out the window for a moment, a smile crossing his face. He continued, "Then Ken came walking down the hall and saw me sitting there. He said, 'Dave, did you hear the news? This place is for sale! They didn't get the grant so they're going to sell it!'"

"Are you kidding?" I asked Dave, in shock at the turn of events.

"No, I'm not. I already went and talked to the manager and she verified what Ken said. It's going to go up for sale soon. The town council will have an open meeting at some point and all bidders are invited to present their plan for use as well as plan for payment. We've got a chance at getting this one!" he concluded, as he sat back in his chair, beaming.

Never in our wildest imaginations could we have put together that scenario.

We'd waited for a year and a half to get in and see the other building, and on the *very day* we find out it's not solid, we get news that Hotel Malenovice is for sale? How did that happen?

We didn't have it yet, but it sure seemed like there was a good shot at it.

Within a few days we found out the details of the town council meeting. It was not going to be easy. There were already two other bidders in line for the hotel. One was the former mayor

of the village. The other was the owner of a large hotel farther up the mountain.

We also found out that the meeting was open to all members of the village, and assumed that the council members would be influenced by townspeople's opinions. Since we were unknown, we wondered how they would respond to outside bidders.

The meeting was in three weeks.

Vladek and Dave worked like crazy on all the documentation for the proposal. It had been of God, most definitely, that our nonprofit status had been approved just weeks earlier, and that we had the authority and proper ability to even make this purchase.

Not only that, we had cash in the bank, ready to release if we were awarded the bid.

But the week prior to the town meeting, Vladek was sick with a fever and couldn't get out of bed. All week we prayed, asking God to restore his health, since he was the only one who could legally represent KAM at the council meeting. We prayed, asking God for mercy over him. Finally, that afternoon he was able to get out of bed and head to the village of Malenovice for the meeting.

When he arrived, it quickly became clear that deals had already been made. Council members had sided with either one of the two other bidders, and Vladek felt outweighed and outnumbered by them.

Each bidder had a set amount of time to give their proposal. Vladek was to be the last one. After the others made their pitch, he stood in front of two hundred-eighty townspeople and members of the council. "I am from a Christian nonprofit organization," he began. "Our plan is to use the hotel as a training

center for youth, to give them moral and spiritual foundations to base their lives on."

He continued with the rest of the proposal, and then concluded with, "We are prepared to pay cash if you award us the bid. Thank you very much for this opportunity." He sat down, unsure of their response.

Vladek expected the council to retire to another room for consultation and consideration of the three proposals. But the mayor called for order right away and said, "Council members, we're taking a vote right now."

He started with the man to his right. "Who will you vote for?" the mayor asked.

"I know I told you I'd vote for you," he said, waving his hand in the direction of one of the other bidders, "but this KAM organization has a better plan. I vote for them."

The next councilman spoke to one of the other bidders. "I know I said I'd support your plan to expand your hotel business up the road, but this man from KAM has a better proposal. I'm going to have to go with it."

Around the room the mayor went, asking for each person's vote while Vladek sat nervously waiting for the final word.

It was unanimous.

"Hotel Malenovice is awarded to KAM!" the mayor announced. "If you pay immediately, you can take possession within thirty days."

And the meeting was adjourned.

Unbelievable!

We were now the owners of the hotel that had been Dave's first choice three years earlier when he'd started looking.

In the weeks following, as paperwork and legalities were taken care of, we found out why the council members had voted unanimously for KAM's proposal. The village was in financial trouble, and we were the only ones who had cash. The other two buyers were going to take out loans.

Had we not raised the money for the other two buildings, we would never have had cash to pay with three weeks' notice. God knew the timing of this, inside and out. He'd had it planned all along.

For weeks, we pinched ourselves to make sure it was real, and talked about what had happened over and over. This was one of the greatest lessons of our lives up to that point. Though the way had not been clear much of the time, we'd continued to follow the Lord, and he had seen us through to the end in his timing and in his way.

In September 1998, for $180,000, we received the building and all the furnishings inside. With the provision of a newly married Czech couple to take over as managers, we were in business just four weeks later.

God's Promise
I will provide every good thing you need to do my will.
Hebrews 13:20-21

CHAPTER TWENTY-FIVE

Troubles and Difficulties

The ache between my eyes, the tremors in my hands, the feeling in the pit of my stomach, the pounding of my heart, the nausea, the knots deep in my neck and the pressure against my chest: all physical manifestations of the pressure we felt in the spiritual realm as we waited on God during those uncertain months prior to buying Hotel Malenovice.

Emotions pressed in as well: fear, doubt, hopelessness, fatigue and discouragement. Many days it was a battle to just keep going, let alone stay faith-filled and trust God while we waited, unsure of the outcome.

And there was a strange thing that happened with Claire's eyes as well.

Shortly after the camp where we first saw the crossing of her eyes, our pediatrician in Czech determined that one of her eyes had spontaneously lost muscular ability to maintain coordination with the other eye. Since it had occurred overnight, the doctor hoped that putting a patch on the good eye would strengthen the muscle on the bad eye and bring it back into realignment.

But after months of the patch, nothing had changed. In fact, it worsened.

There were other difficulties during that time as well. Caleb, our middle son who was just five years old, began to experience night terrors on a regular basis. It was not unusual to have him awaken between 2 and 3 a.m., screaming. One, or both of us, would go to his room to quiet, soothe and comfort him until he went back to sleep. While it didn't usually take more than ten to fifteen minutes, it was exhausting night after night.

Tyler, our oldest, a third-grader at the time, contracted a severe case of mononucleosis.

I had a miscarriage of our fourth child, and spent time in the United States trying to solve a fatigue issue that plagued me for a year.

While any one of those occurrences can be normal and explainable, it was the accumulation of difficulties and pressure that was so wearing. Many of those days, even years, are "lost." We lived in a fog, just trying to survive day to day.

But a movement of God among the youth was taking place, and even in those foggy, stressful days, we didn't lose sight of that.

Stories of young people coming to know Jesus brought no end of joy as we saw them put their faith in Christ, and begin to live it out despite opposition from family and friends. Watching their eyes open to spiritual truth, and the transformation it brought in their lives, renewed our strength and energy as we pressed forward despite difficulties.

By the fall of 1999, after many doctor visits and several trips to the States for consultations and therapy, it was determined that Claire needed surgery to correct her eye. She and I flew to Chicago just days after her fifth birthday, and spent nearly four weeks there as she endured not just one, but two surgeries.

During the week after the first surgery, I agonized over the pain Claire seemed to be experiencing post-op, and finally called her doctor to see if it was normal. He asked me to bring her to his office, and then found she had contracted a bacterial infection in the eye, which required another surgery.

I remember sitting on her bed the night before going back to the hospital, holding her in my arms, as I was about to deliver the news. Not wanting to cause unnecessary anxiety, I'd waited until then to tell her she'd be going back into the hospital for another surgery in the morning.

"But Mommy, why?" she sobbed in my arms.

We both cried again in the early morning as I woke her just in time to leave for surgery. It was one of the saddest mornings I'd ever experienced.

The first surgery corrected the crossing of her eyes, and the second one took care of the infection. A few weeks later when her doctor gave the "all clear," we were able to return home to Czech and resume life there.

Over the next ten years, we saw her doctor every time we were in Chicago, to see if the surgery held. Her eye muscle strengthened over time, and eventually she even outgrew the nearsightedness that had occurred when her eyes had crossed.

When she was sixteen, her doctor pronounced her well and said he didn't need to see her again, unless she had any other problems. What a blessing he was to us for all those years Claire was under his care.

We often wondered what role the spiritual dimension played in that event of our lives, as well as the other difficulties we encountered during those early years. Was the Lord refining us? Was Satan trying to knock us off course? Probably yes and yes.

At the time, we rolled through them as best as we could.

But it certainly wasn't the last time that we experienced health difficulties that coincided with significant thrusts forward in the ministry.

Between the fall of 1998 and August 2000, more camps were added in the summers as hundreds of students heard the gospel, and training events were packed with young leaders eager to learn.

We held as many of those camps and training events at Hotel Malenovice as we could, and brought our growing team there for retreats and holidays. We also offered it to churches across the country for use as well.

But it was in great need of renovation and expansion. We exceeded its capacities many times, wishing for more space. Through the generosity of literally thousands of individuals, churches and foundations, we were able to shut Hotel Malenovice down in the fall of 2000 and begin renovation.

We went up and over and out, literally encasing the old frame in a new one. We added balconies and a whole new floor for more hotel rooms and meeting space. We expanded the dining area and built a large meeting area for 160 people. With a project finish date of August 2001, we were excited about the

next phase of Josiah Venture's ministry, and what God wanted to do through this important place.

But in the middle of the renovation and expansion project, we experienced another family difficulty. Claire, now six, began to wilt. Every time we turned around, she was sick: coughs, sore throats, infections, skin problems, headaches, lack of energy, tiredness or stomach pain. If it wasn't one thing, it was another.

She and I visited our Czech pediatrician regularly, trying to figure out why she couldn't stay well. We tried all sorts of remedies, prescriptions and therapies to help her, but to no avail. She seemed to be slipping away from us.

Then the vomiting started. Something seemed to be terribly wrong.

Dave was in the midst of Malenovice's reconstruction, working alongside our project manager and the firm we'd hired to do most of the work. The early winter snow we usually get in the Beskydy Mountains held off that year until the roof was on in January. Progress on the building proceeded at a rapid pace.

Yet our daughter was losing ground, week by week, day by day.

After unsuccessful attempts to solve the mystery in Czech, Dave and I decided I should take Claire to Chicago and try to see some doctors who could find out what was going on.

We arrived in mid-April to the home of some friends. Claire lay on their couch, listless, for several days, while I made phone calls to doctors, trying to find someone to help us. On the third day, she spiked a high fever, and after a call to one of the doctors who told me to take her to the emergency room, we left for the

hospital. After a quick exam in the ER, she was admitted and began treatment for what seemed like a kidney infection.

As I watched her drift in and out of sleep, barely able to talk in the first twenty-four hours, I wondered if we were on the verge of something even worse. It was terrifying to be there alone, with no easy way to contact Dave and unsure of what news would come the next day.

She responded to the antibiotics, and with no further testing, was discharged three days later. I was relieved on one hand, but still troubled as the listlessness and other symptoms persisted. It was frustrating to see that something was wrong with Claire, but be unable to find someone to help me get to the bottom of it. While the treatment for her kidney infection brought healing there, it was only a small part of what she was experiencing.

A week later, at the suggestion of a friend, I made an appointment with another doctor, who was known for his thorough exams. He spent several hours with us, not only giving her a physical exam, but also asking extensive questions. He asked me to fill out a long questionnaire and document as much information as I could remember about Claire's health history and our lives.

After completing his comprehensive exam, he asked if I could come into his office while Claire waited with a friend out in the waiting room.

"I have some good news and bad news," he began. "While I can see that your daughter is indeed quite ill, I don't think what she's dealing with is life threatening. That's the good news."

I breathed a little easier.

"Now for the bad news," he continued. "I think your daughter is reacting to, if not allergic to, the house you're living in."

I sat across from him, shocked, unable to speak. "Why would you say that?" I finally asked.

"Well, it's just a gut feeling. But I've seen this before, especially in kids. When they're not thriving, and especially when they've lived in the same house their whole life, it tells me that something isn't necessarily wrong with their body, as it is with how their body responds to the environment or actual house they're living in.

"For instance, kids with severe asthma shouldn't be living in an environment with heavy air pollution or high pollen levels. I tell parents, if it is at all possible, to take a serious look at where they're living. If a simple—though I realize it's never simple—change of environment would bring help to their child, then they should do whatever is possible to make a move.

"You told me about the city you live in, the pollution levels there, what the environment is like that Claire has grown up in, where your house is situated and how old it is. You've told me about Claire's symptoms, and I can even see some of them, but because all her tests come back negative—which you should be glad for—it tells me that this is probably environmental."

"So you're saying that Claire could be sick because of our house?" I asked incredulously.

"Yes, I am. I've seen it many times in my thirty-five years of practice. Our fields of medicine are so specialized these days that sometimes we forget to come up out of the trees and look at the forest to find what's wrong. In your case, looking at the

forest may mean that Claire is simply unable to tolerate the house or area that you're in.

"I don't think it's too late for her, though. I think a move, perhaps out into the country where the air quality is better, and the house is newer, could make all the difference in her health. You really should consider this."

I didn't know what to say. Finally finding my voice, I said, "You don't understand: there is no way we can move from our house."

I'd already explained to him that our house functioned as the center for the ministry. "If we moved, where would all of that go?" I asked, realizing he probably didn't have any answer to my question.

He sat back, and with a shrug of his shoulders said, "Well, we're talking about your daughter's life."

With piercing eyes, he continued, "I suggest you do everything you can to find out if it is indeed a problem with your house that's impacting her. And if it is, you'll have to decide which is more important: the ministry or your daughter."

God's Promise
Don't worry; I will take care of you.
Matthew 6:25-26

CHAPTER TWENTY-SIX

Walking Away

I ached over this news for days. Could it really be that our house was making Claire sick? And if so, how? What was it in the house that caused her to suffer so much?

It made sense. The longer we were in the States, the healthier she got. After six weeks there, she had color in her cheeks again, many (though not all) of the symptoms were gone and she was happier than she'd been in months.

I wondered, *How am I going to tell Dave that the best solution I've come up with to Claire's health problems is to leave our house and go somewhere else?*

I waited until we returned to Czech to give him that news.

The evening after we arrived home, he and I sat in our living room and I shared all the doctor had told me.

"But we can't do that," Dave said, responding just as I had when talking with the doctor. "How could he know that there is

something wrong with our house? We can't just sell it based on a doctor's gut feeling."

"I know," I replied, "but it does make sense. She got better when we went away from here."

"Yes, but she seems to be doing fine now that she's back. Maybe it was just that kidney infection, and she's really okay now. Can you imagine how difficult everything would be if we had to move? And we don't even know if it's the house that caused the problem. Let's wait and see how she does before we make any decisions," Dave concluded.

But over the next two weeks, we watched Claire deteriorate once again. Most of the symptoms returned and she spent her time on the couch or in bed, unable to go to school. Words can't begin to describe how excruciating it was to watch our daughter wilt away in front of our eyes. I began asking the Lord, "Why?" many times throughout each day.

"Lord, you brought us here to do your work. Why are you making it so difficult for us?"

"God, you healed people in the Bible, why won't you heal our little girl?"

"We're in the middle of the biggest thrust forward for your kingdom's sake. Why would you bring this difficulty right now?"

"Why couldn't you have brought this difficulty at a different time? This is too hard."

In April, shortly before Claire and I left for Chicago, Dave's brother, Steve, brought a group of students on a spring break trip from Multnomah University. A professor there, he liked to bring students from his youth ministry/educational department to see possibilities outside the United States where they could use their gifts and skills. We hosted two of his students at our house through the weekend, and bonded with one of them in a very short time.

Becca McMartin, a missionary kid and TCK (third culture kid), had grown up in Haiti. Now a senior at Multnomah, there was something in the way she related to our kids that was so endearing. As I watched her playing with them, catching them in her arms as they thrust themselves off the couch, and burying them in a hug, I was drawn to her and wanted to hang out with her myself.

After feeling prompted by the Lord, I wrote to Becca after she'd gone back to the States and simply said, "I don't know what you're doing this summer, but we'd love to have you come and live with us. Our kids enjoyed you and we did too. I don't really know what I'm offering, or why you'd even want to come, but I just had to write and ask."

I heard back from her soon afterward with a nice note saying, "Thanks, but I'm in several weddings this summer and couldn't miss them. But I enjoyed you guys too!"

Oddly, I was disappointed to get that news. There was something that compelled me to pray anyway, that if God meant for Becca to come, she'd change her mind.

She did.

Soon afterward she wrote me back and said, "I don't know why, but I think I'm supposed to come." When I asked about her friends' weddings, she said, "They'll understand if I tell them that the Lord wants me to do this."

We moved forward with plans for her to come for the summer.

Soon after arriving back from Chicago, it was clear that Claire was not doing well again. My mom told me about a doctor friend who had connections to the Lucile Packard Children's Hospital at Stanford in California. He told my mom he was willing to contact a friend there and ask for help on our behalf.

Within two days, we had the green light from his friend, the head doctor in neonatal care. While his specialty was preemie babies, he felt confident that someone on his hospital staff would be able to figure out the mystery of a little girl from the Czech Republic.

Then Becca arrived. Her ticket had been purchased weeks earlier, but as God would arrange it, she arrived just in time, before Claire and I left to seek help in California.

Dave was already in the States, speaking at a mission's conference for one of our supporting churches in Colorado. Before he left, he'd settled Claire, the boys and me into a small rented apartment to test the theory that our house was causing Claire problems. The fevers and vomiting stopped, but the other symptoms persisted. So when the opportunity came to get help at Stanford, we took it.

Becca arrived on Friday night and spent the night with us at the apartment. I had just received word that we could go to Stanford, so I proposed to her the wildest of wild ideas on her first night in the Czech Republic.

"Becca, I don't know how to tell you this, but I've got to leave with Claire on Sunday to go to the children's hospital and try to get help for her. Dave's supposed to come home on Monday, but he will change his flight and come meet me there. Can you stay with the boys and take care of them while we're gone?"

Yes, it was a crazy request. She'd been in country all of a few hours and suddenly had kids and a household to run. I was so thankful that she was up for it, knowing that God had sent her for this reason.

Saturday I moved us all back home to our house, even though I knew Claire would not feel well. But I had to pack and give Becca all the instructions in just a little more than twenty-four hours. I also had to spend time with Tyler and Caleb (ages ten and eight), explaining what was about to happen. It was a good thing they liked Becca, even though they barely knew her.

Early Sunday morning, Laura drove from Poland to pick us up. Saying goodbye to the boys was agonizing. I cried as we pulled out of the driveway and headed for the airport in Vienna, not knowing when I would see them, or what would happen between that moment and whenever we'd come home.

Becca, Tyler and Caleb stood in the driveway, shoeless and in pajamas, waving us off. I didn't find out until much later that the front door had closed as we all stood on the driveway saying goodbye, locking them out for a while after we left. I'm glad I didn't know. I had enough on my mind as we headed to Vienna to catch a flight to Los Angeles.

Even though we'd only spent one week at our house since returning from Chicago, Claire was not doing well: lethargic, weak, with bouts of nausea, vomiting and fevers. It was excruciating to watch and not be able to do anything for her.

In our one week at home, I thought to measure and weigh her to compare it against where she'd been a year earlier. I was shocked at what I found. No growth, no weight gained. She

was exactly the same as she'd been for a year. Again, something seemed to be wrong with our girl. I contemplated all these things as we flew to the West Coast.

Friends met us at the San Jose airport after a long flight, much of which Claire spent sleeping. They brought a car to loan to me during our time in California, and I drove off feeling overwhelmed by the generosity and care of people at such a time of need.

I also felt scared by what the doctors at this world-class children's hospital might find in Claire.

Barely able to sleep, I wrestled through the night with the Lord, asking him for answers about what was going on in our little girl's body. If someone had told me that Claire would be sick for twelve months, I probably could've endured it. It was the not knowing that wore down my emotions and faith.

I clung to the Word, as the sun rose and I could read in the dim light. "He who dwells in the shelter of the Most High will rest in the shadow of the Almighty. I will say of the Lord, 'He is my refuge and my fortress, my God, in whom I trust'" (Psalm 91:1-2).

"Lord," I called out, "I am really trying to trust you and believe that you're my refuge. But I feel exposed and weak right now. Please help me in my weakness."

Following him was difficult when I didn't know where we were going. But with everything in me, I sought to put myself under his shelter and walk daily with him through whatever circumstances arose.

Dave arrived from Colorado the next day, with news that arrangements had been made through friends for us to stay with

a woman, recently widowed. Only three weeks after losing her husband, she opened her home and gave us a small cottage out back to stay in for as long as we needed. It was a peaceful refuge.

Appointments began at the hospital, with many tests and procedures. The doctors, nurses and all personnel treated us kindly and helpfully as we navigated the hospital system. For one particularly difficult test, Claire was given one of the popular Beanie Babies of the day to help her endure it. Kindness upon kindness extended to us as we proceeded through the system.

Finally, after three weeks of waiting, we went in to see the doctor for the results of all the testing.

"While we can see that your daughter is ill, there is nothing significant in the test results to indicate what is wrong. She has a few minor imbalances in her blood work, and needs an antibiotic to clear that up. But otherwise, she's fine."

And honestly, after three weeks in California, she *was* much better. Again, she had color in her cheeks, many of the symptoms had lessened, and she was her happy self again.

I, on the other hand, was frustrated. It was wonderful to see her beginning to return to her old self, but I wondered what would happen when we returned home. Would the symptoms come back; would she again have high fevers and vomiting? Would she begin to thrive, or continue her downward spiral in Czech?

One afternoon while she played a game with Suzanne, the woman who had taken us into her home, Dave and I sat outside on the steps, talking about what to do. The construction and renovation of Hotel Malenovice was entering an important

stage, and Dave felt he needed to be back for it. Already gone for three weeks, he knew he was needed there. Then there were the boys and Becca, waiting at home for at least one parent to arrive.

"I think I need to get back to Czech," Dave gently said as he held my hand. "The doctor said he wanted to run a few more tests before letting her go. Can you handle those without me?"

I didn't want to, but I knew I needed to. While he was right about needing to go home, I needed to stay to finish every possible test. I wanted to make sure we weren't missing something, so I agreed to stay with Claire.

"And listen, if you get back and all her symptoms return, we will not stop pursuing what's wrong. I want you to know that *nothing* is more important than her and her health, even if it means leaving Czech. We are not going to sacrifice our daughter for the sake of ministry. I don't believe that's God's heart or intention for us. So just know that, okay?" he said as he wiped tears from my face.

With his reassurance, and the Lord's sheltering protection over us, we said goodbye to him the next day as he headed home.

Claire and I stayed for another week, finishing up the last tests and getting the results.

Negative.

As far as one of the best children's hospitals in the world could tell, nothing was wrong with Claire.

She and I returned home to happy hugs from the boys and Becca. They'd been there three weeks without a parent, four weeks without me. Her presence with them was an invaluable gift to us, and brought much-needed stability into their lives at that critical time. But they were all glad to see us come back home.

The very next morning reality struck. Claire began to vomit and the fever returned.

"Lord!" I cried out. "What are you doing?"

Claire managed to go to her last day of first grade and participated in the closing ceremonies of the school year. That afternoon she was back on the couch, pale and listless as if she'd never left home.

It was the oddest thing to observe. I'd just been with her in California and watched her swim in a pool, dance in new ballet clothes, play games with Suzanne and eat raspberries like they were candy, and yet now, she lay on the couch with no appetite and no energy. Her hair hung limp, and her skin became translucent. We'd only been home three days.

Two days after school had ended, I asked Dave to look at her. She'd just vomited, and her temperature was 101.

He quietly said, "I think it's time to leave."

"To where?" I asked, trying to keep my voice down so it didn't alarm her.

"I honestly don't know. But it seems this house is slowly killing her. We've got to leave and get her away. I think we should go up into the mountains and plan on staying there for the summer to see if it makes a difference. Let me go make a few phone calls, but if you can, start packing."

While she drifted off to sleep, which happened often during these sick episodes, I gathered the boys and Becca together in the kitchen and told them what was happening.

"Dad says we need to leave the house for Claire's sake. I don't know for how long, and I don't know where we're going. But we need to pack your bags with clothes, and you need to choose a few books and toys to put into another bag. We'll see if we can bring your bikes with us. Dad wants to leave this afternoon."

Privately to Becca I said, "I'm so thankful you're here right now. God led you to be with us for this time—thank you for listening to him and coming. I don't know what's next. I'm glad you're in this with us."

An hour later we packed our van and headed off to the mountains. I didn't know where we were going.

God's Promise
I will save you in the midst of your troubles.
Psalm 138:7

CHAPTER TWENTY-SEVEN

Suffering and Change

There are certain times in your life where it feels like the curtain is pulled back and you are allowed a peek into God's bigger picture. Although you might not know the significance of the moment, you still are aware that something important is happening.

That's how I felt that day as we drove off to the mountains.

It didn't feel like just an ordinary getaway or family vacation. It felt like something was shifting in our lives, and that we'd never be the same because of it.

I hoped and prayed that it was not leading us toward something worse with Claire. But I had to acknowledge during that drive that it could be. Though we were taking her away from our home, which seemed to be poisoning her, I didn't know if we were too late.

Only time would tell.

Dave and I talked quietly up front, while Becca told the kids stories in the back of the van as we drove into the mountains. Forty-five minutes later we arrived at an old hotel up past our own Hotel Malenovice.

We checked into the tired old hotel rooms and slept fitfully that night as Claire continued to suffer from a high fever. A few days later we were able to move down the hill into Ken and Andrea's house, our JV teammates, while they went on vacation for a week. Claire's fever subsided, but she was tired and achy for the following days at their house.

Rain poured down the entire week. I felt as though heaven was crying for me.

Everything in my body hurt as we sat inside that week trying to find things to do. I think it was more emotional hurt than it was physical. But still, it was a painful time. I wanted it to be over so badly. Time and time again, I cried out to the Lord to save us, to protect us, to do something.

And slowly, ever so slowly, Claire began to come back to life.

She and Caleb suffered a terrible round of strep throat that summer, and we all spent a lot of time inside. But I watched her gain ground.

After a week at our teammates' house, Dave arranged for us to move into Hotel Malenovice, even though it was still in the midst of renovation. One of the upstairs family rooms with six beds was finished, so we moved everybody into it. Eventually, Becca moved into a room down a floor, but spent her time with us in our room each day.

It was one of the longest summers we ever endured.

I turned forty that summer, and for my birthday, Dave, the kids and Becca arranged a wonderful day of all my favorite things: gifts, meals out, massage and an adventure. It meant the world to me to forget our troubles for a day.

Excited, the kids blindfolded me for my adventure before leaving the hotel. We drove to an undisclosed location, amid much giggling and chatter from the kids. They led me out onto pavement, and I had no idea where we were. The kids could hardly contain their excitement before pulling off the blindfold.

I found myself at the little local airport in the village of Malenovice. Dave had arranged for us to go up in a sightseeing plane as my big birthday surprise. "You need to get a little perspective," he said with a grin.

After nervously stepping into the four-seater plane, I waved goodbye to the kids and Becca. The flight over the mountains was breathtaking, and I actually enjoyed it much more than I expected. It truly was good to get "up" and take a look down. It was as if God was letting me see his view for a few minutes. I nearly heard him whisper in my ear over the roar of the plane's engine, "This is what I see from my view … I see it all."

Just days earlier I had written in my journal, "When will you show us where to go? I can't see the way."

"I see it all." Those were comforting words that I needed to hear while up in the plane.

Dave left several days later for leadership meetings in Budapest with our mission organization. With Claire steadily gaining ground, the kids and I packed the van for a family vacation while Dave was at his meetings.

We'd been going to Croatia for three summers, camping near the beach in Baška, on the island of Krk. However, with all that had been happening, I told Dave I didn't think I could camp that year. So we'd decided to head to another beach town on the mainland and find an apartment.

The kids and I happily drove to Vienna a few days later to meet Dave. I was looking forward to a week in our favorite vacation country. But when we picked Dave up, I knew something was wrong.

"Let's just get in the van and start driving. The kids will fall asleep soon and then we can talk," Dave quietly said as he greeted us.

While the kids happily chattered in the back, we talked about other things, like the opening of the newly renovated Hotel Malenovice that had taken place just before he'd left for Budapest. Friends had booked the hotel in faith a year earlier, in anticipation of its opening, to host a conference for Eastern European graduates of Wheaton College's summer school program.

As the last of the carpet was laid in the meeting room, Christian leaders from all over Central and Eastern Europe were arriving for our first conference held in the newly renovated hotel. It was a thrilling time as we saw the completion of it after six years of dreaming, planning and executing the vision.

The ongoing internship program that had started in the garage of our house in Havířov was another topic as we drove. In its fourth year by that time, it would move up to Hotel Malenovice from our house and have the largest class yet. Dave was excited about the leaders who were going to study for the year.

Finally, as the dusky sky turned to darkness and the kids nodded off to sleep in the back of the van, Dave said, "It's been a difficult couple of days at those meetings. I don't know how to ease into this except to start by telling you: It looks like we have to start our own mission organization."

God's Promise
You will have perfect peace if you keep focused on me.
Isaiah 26:3

CHAPTER TWENTY-EIGHT

Birth of a Mission

When we started Josiah Venture, our heart was to reach the youth of Central and Eastern Europe. We wanted to live on the mission field to personally be part of that vision, not run a mission agency from the United States. Because of that, it was essential to find an organization with a similar vision, willing to host us as a team within a team.

God led us to an innovative, like-minded organization, and we served up until that time under their umbrella. Dave and I were able to stay in Czech, directly involved in ministry, and the organization took care of administrative support. Our JV team grew to thirty-three, and new team members were in the process of raising support to begin ministry in Slovenia, our fourth country with JV staff.

But at the meetings in Budapest, it became apparent that it was time for us to begin Josiah Venture as its own mission organization.

Running an organization was the last thing we wanted to do, but in order to grow, we knew it was a necessary step. Dave left for Chicago in September to talk through how and when this would take place.

It was the morning of September 11, 2001, when he was in the offices of our partner organization to talk through the transition. The first televised reports of the devastating terrorist attack that became known as 9/11 brought great shock and sorrow. It was hard to believe that on a day when such evil had taken place in our home country, God was orchestrating the details of Josiah Venture to become a nonprofit mission organization in Europe.

Somehow in God's economy, there was significance to the dichotomy of events that day.

Dave called a classmate from Wheaton College, who had expertise in the nonprofit world, and they met the next day. "I know a lawyer who wrote the codes for the Illinois 501(c)(3) laws. I think she can help you with that process. And my partners and I have been thinking about starting a new section of our company to provide back services for small organizations like yours. You could be our first client," he told Dave in his office.

Only God could put those details together.

The next week was spent in back-to-back meetings trying to set everything in motion for the forming of Josiah Venture as a nonprofit, self-standing mission organization. Dave met with lawyers and completed reams of forms, as well as created a board of directors before he left the States. Key people in our lives at the time, including our pastor at Grace Church and Dann Spader, the head of Sonlife, agreed to serve on the board.

It was an intense time in Dave's life, at the same time as it was intense throughout our nation.

The day he flew back to Czech, he had one final meeting in downtown Chicago. All the new board members came to sign paperwork that would allow our lawyer to file for 501(c)(3) status with the state of Illinois. She said she would do everything she could to see that the status would be approved by the end of the year. We asked God to do a miracle and grant us our needed status so that we could seamlessly transition from the old organization to the new one on January 1, 2002.

The months that followed were a steady stream of activity as we headed toward becoming our own organization; we spent hours together talking, praying, wrestling, and seeking God's wisdom as we looked forward into the future of Josiah Venture.

One of the key moves was making a way to allow nationals to be full partners in what we were doing. We set it up so there could be national partner organizations in each of the countries. Nationally led, not as subsidiaries, but as full partners, this allowed our national staff to rise into significant leadership, take ownership for the movement in their country, raise money locally and bring on new staff from within a country.

The Josiah Venture Council was formed at that time as well. Two representatives from each country, a national and a missionary, would serve as "elders" to the organization and provide leadership to the whole.

We organized things in an efficient and effective way, providing quality services to our people at a lower cost than before. We also clarified our vision and decided on the key values for

JV: bold faith, dynamic community, God-honoring excellence, deep integrity and indigenous empowerment.

After having been part of a large organization with a variety of emphases, we were now able to clearly articulate our values and mission, as well as structure ourselves for growth into the future.

Dave sought to create the new Josiah Venture organization as a lean and effective one. He wanted most of the organization's energy deployed on the front lines rather than in the back office, and wanted to ensure that we did all we could to make the most impact for Christ.

In December, we learned that our 501(c)(3) had been granted in record time. By the end of the month, Cedarstone, our friends' business, completed all their new systems in order to transition accounting over from the other organization.

On January 1, 2002, Josiah Venture went "live" as a mission organization.

God's Promise
I will not let you fall for I am watching over you day and night.
Psalm 121:3

CHAPTER TWENTY-NINE Long Awaited Answers

While Dave worked on putting together a new mission organization over the fall months, I tried to provide a steadiness in our family after all we'd been through in the spring and summer. But it was not easy.

For the month of September, I drove the kids back and forth to school in Havířov and spent my days at our house. For the first week after the attack of 9/11, I was glued to my computer in horror, watching the suffering my fellow Americans were enduring.

We also realized that whatever was present in the house was still deadly to Claire. If she spent so much as ten minutes at the house after school, she became ill. By the end of the month, it became evident that it would not be possible for us to move back.

Ever.

The doctor in Chicago had been right: there was something poisonous to Claire in our house, and we could not subject

her to it any longer. We suspected that the problem was mold, which was prevalent in many houses in the area, especially the older ones that were for rent or for sale.

We searched for other housing in the area surrounding Hotel Malenovice, but could find nothing that was clean enough for Claire except the hotel itself. In fact, when we took her to look at a few possibilities, she became ill immediately.

After much prayer, we decided to take the kids out of school in Havířov and transfer them to the nearby school in Frýdlant nad Ostravicí, while continuing to live in the hotel. The little efficiency apartment that was meant for the caretaker was finished by the end of the month, and we moved in on October 6, 2001.

Two days later, the kids started school. It was Claire's seventh birthday. That night, after a little party with JV friends, all three kids cried as they lay in their beds. Dave and I felt like crying too. It had been a long, hard road, and we couldn't see the end of it.

Kneeling beside their beds, all squished together in one room, we cried out to the Lord again to protect and lead us. Each of us was desperate for him in our own way.

Becca McMartin stayed on that fall, though the original plan had only included the summer. I don't know what we would've done without her had she not stayed. She taught English in town, which provided her with the means to stay. When she wasn't teaching, she was with us, telling stories, playing games, being silly and giving herself as a friend to all of us.

Toward the end of January, Caleb began to complain of stomach pain. Many people had the flu that winter, so we assumed he picked it up as well. But by mid-February, his pain

had not gone away. Some days he could make it to school, but others found him doubled over and unable to even stand up.

We took a short trip for the kids' mid-winter break and headed to Slovenia where Dave's brother, Josh, and his family, had moved the previous May to begin ministry with JV. Anxious to see their world and connect with them, everyone looked forward to the trip.

But on our way to the ski slope one afternoon, Caleb suddenly vomited. The pain in his stomach seemed worse than usual. He cried and told us he was trying to be brave, but that he was hurting again.

As soon as we returned to Czech, we took him to the doctor to get help.

None of the traditional remedies brought relief. By late March, Caleb was spending most every day lying in our living room with headphones over his ears to distract him, and a hot water bottle on his stomach to give the tiniest amount of relief. He missed over a month of school.

I was frustrated. It was obvious something was wrong, but none of the doctors we visited seemed to take it seriously enough to pursue more in-depth testing to find out what was going on. Many nights I pleaded with the Lord to do something, anything. Caleb's pain was exhausting to him, and also to the rest of the family.

Dave could see that I was on the brink of emotional collapse, so arranged for Becca to come stay with the kids for an evening while we went out for dinner.

Living up at the hotel had its ups and downs. The peaceful, serene setting of the mountains brought a balm to all of

our souls as we watched and enjoyed the constant change of weather from our balcony window.

But there were also challenges. When it snowed, or became icy, the road was impassible. This meant parking alongside the road below, hoping that no passing cars would run into our parked cars. It also meant numerous hikes up and down the hill as I drove back and forth to school, according to the kids' various schedules and lessons. Then there was the hike up with groceries most every day. I was definitely more fit than I'd ever been before.

One evening, when Dave and I headed out for a date night, we were able to drive our car down the mountain, as there'd been a melt earlier in the day. It seemed as though spring was on its way.

Although Caleb was still experiencing pain, I let the burden of it slip off that evening as we sat in a restaurant and talked, enjoying each other's company for hours. By the time we headed for home, I felt refreshed and ready to step back into dealing with Caleb's situation.

A few minutes later, as we headed up the hill toward the hotel, Dave suddenly, and uncharacteristically, yelled at me. "Get out!" he cried with a terror in his voice that I'd never heard.

Asking no questions, I flung open the door of our Czech-made Škoda and hurled myself out, barely slamming the door as my feet met the black ice beneath me. While I fell to the ground, the car rolled backward with Dave in it, crashing over an embankment.

I watched in horror as the lights of the car barreled away from me, and heard the cracking of trees, the shattering of glass and the thud as it came to a stop.

In the cold night air, I didn't know if Dave was alive or not.

Most of us have at least one moment of terror in our lives. You never forget it. You also don't forget the thoughts that race through your mind when it happens. Those thoughts are usually telling. As I watched Dave plunge over the edge, I thought to myself, *I will praise the Lord, even if he dies.*

It surprised me. I'd always wondered how I would respond in such a moment. There was honestly something comforting in that split second of knowing that I'd turn to the Lord, and that I knew his grace would be enough even if the worst happened.

But then I heard it.

Laughter. Huge, sparkling, delightful laughter.

It was Dave, laughing from the front seat of the car!

Sliding and slipping, I cautiously made my way down the hill and over to the edge of the embankment. There I saw the tree behind the car that held him from going completely over.

And there was Dave in the driver's seat, laughing.

"What else could possibly happen to us?" he laughingly cried out.

Able to open the door, he crawled out through the glass and we embraced there on the side of the hill, excruciatingly grateful for our lives.

It was late and with no way to get help, there was nothing that could be done until morning. We walked hand in hand up the road to the hotel where we made our way inside, told Becca what happened and climbed into our beds to sleep.

The next morning Dave made a call to the police in town, as we knew that we'd need a report in order to make a claim to our insurance. Their response shocked us.

"There will be a fine for not reporting this incident," the policeman harshly told Dave at the scene of our one-car accident.

"But no one else was involved. And it was late at night!" Dave protested.

"I'm sorry, but it's the law," the officer declared.

Paying the expensive fine was not fun. But we thanked God anyway, knowing it was a small price to pay considering what had happened. Insurance took care of repairing the car, which remarkably, was not totaled.

It wasn't long before the shock of that event was eclipsed by the deterioration of Caleb.

He'd already spent a week in the hospital as the doctors tried to determine what was causing the pain. But with each passing day, it became worse. One night, when the pain seemed to be intolerable, we rushed him to the emergency room.

Another round of ultrasounds, CT scans and MRIs produced nothing. The next afternoon, the head of the children's ward asked to meet with us.

"I'd like to order a psychiatric workup for you and your son," he said matter-of-factly. Before we could even speak, he continued, "We've done everything we can to find the source of his pain, but it appears to me that it is psychosomatic, and my guess is that something is going on in your family that is causing him to react and experience phantom pain."

As I quietly began to cry, Dave tried to protest and explain that this was not the case, and that we still believed something was physically wrong with him.

The doctor persisted and told us to come in the next day to set up the appointments.

I felt like we were living in a nightmare.

"Why are you doing this to us, God?" I harshly cried to him. "All we've done is try to serve you and this is what we get?"

I wasn't a pretty sight as we left Caleb in the hospital and went home that night. In agony, I begged the Lord to do something for Caleb to relieve his pain. I wrestled through the night with God's sovereignty and his goodness, doubting his love and plan for us all.

By morning, I was exhausted.

Then the phone rang.

"In the night as I was thinking about your son, I had another thought," the doctor said cautiously. "I'd like to get him in for exploratory laparoscopic surgery. Can you be here immediately? There is an opening in the OR at ten and I'd like to take it, but we need you here to sign papers."

We could hardly believe our ears, feeling a sense of panic, yet relief. We raced back to the hospital in time to sign the papers and see our nine-year-old Caleb wheeled in for surgery, his eyes wide and scared.

Sitting outside the OR, in a dull waiting area that was nothing more than a hallway where doctors, nurses and orderlies passed by, we prayed like we'd never prayed before.

An hour after they took him in, that doctor came out in his scrubs, his mask dangling from around his neck. "We've found it. We know what's wrong. I don't have time to explain, but I need your permission to operate. We're going to take out part of his intestines that have died."

God's Promise
I watch over you and I listen for your prayers.
Psalm 34:15

CHAPTER THIRTY Surrender and Provision

Never in my life had I heard the word "intussuscep-tion." But that's what had occurred in Caleb's stom-ach, or more precisely, his intestines.

Intussusception is a serious condition in which part of the intestine telescopes into an adjacent part of the intestine, like a sock being turned inside out. This "telescoping" often blocks food or fluid from passing through and cuts off blood supply to the part of the intestine that's affected, which can lead to a tear in the bowel.

If it remains in the telescoped position, the condition is usually fatal within days.

During the evening after our conversation, the doctor had remembered a case he'd seen years earlier, where a young man experienced similar symptoms. Because this condition nor-mally occurs only in young babies and the elderly, it's not con-sidered in the diagnostic process. Surely only God's prompting

had brought the possibility to his mind the very night before he wanted to submit Caleb to psychiatric testing.

The doctor told us after surgery that a section of Caleb's intestines looked like they belonged to an eighty-year-old man, not a nine-year-old boy. They removed eighteen inches (forty-five centimeters) of deteriorated intestines that day, thus saving his life.

Our relief was immense.

Dave stayed with him round the clock at the hospital for the next week. His recovery was difficult and painful, both physically and emotionally, so he needed someone present at all times.

In the midst of demanding circumstances, there was a sweetness of bonding that occurred between Dave and Caleb. Unlike years earlier when Dave slept in a storage closet at the hospital after Caleb broke his leg, he was able to not only stay in the room during the day, but at night as well. They spent day and night together as Caleb's body healed from surgery and months of pain.

When Caleb returned home two weeks after he had entered the hospital, we all took deep breaths of relief and praised the Lord that in the eleventh hour, he'd come through with a solution.

However, I continued to struggle with my emotions toward the Lord.

Why couldn't you have prevented this?

Why did it have to last so long?

Why are you doing this to us?

Why did Caleb have to go through this?

Why don't you care?

Why, Why, Why, I repeatedly asked.

I was angry with God. I felt like he unnecessarily caused infliction on Caleb and on us. It seemed unfair, unkind and ultimately, unloving.

I stomped my way through life for the next weeks as I tried to pull our lives back together.

I hired a tutor so Caleb could complete third grade. I cared for his incision and helped him through recovery at home. I cooked meals once again for our family. I tried to read my Bible. I tried to pray.

But I was mad.

One Saturday afternoon, Dave came into the kitchen. As I banged dishes around in the sink, he gently tried to talk to me. "It's not helping anything by being mad about what's happened," he said as I continued to wash with my back turned to him. "You keep asking God for a 'why' and I don't think he's going to give it to you. He doesn't need to."

I whirled around and lashed back at him, "Why can't we know why? It doesn't make sense to me. Why won't God show us what he's doing? If I knew why, I could endure it."

I glared at him, as if it were his fault.

Dave tenderly replied, "I think he's doing this to teach us to not need to ask that question—in fact, to stop asking it. He's not required to tell us why. Even if he did, we wouldn't understand. He's asking us to trust him without knowing why."

I threw the dish towel at him—something I'd never done before.

"Well, you might trust him, but I *don't*." And with that I ran into our room, slammed the door, locked it and fell across our bed, weeping hot, desperate tears.

I was so tired of all that we'd endured over the years. I wanted someone to blame for how hard it had been. And I wanted to know why God wouldn't answer why.

While we'd had answers from him along the way, it was always only just enough to get by. There had rarely been long-term solutions or satisfactory answers to my questions, and I was tired of that.

Lying on our bed, I sobbed and sobbed that day. I cried until there were no more tears. And then I cried some more. It was gut-wrenching, and I felt like my heart was going to break into pieces. I kept pounding on the bed and calling out, *Why, God? Why won't you answer me? Why are you making this so hard? Why?*

Several hours went by. I'd never had such a terrifying, agonizing battle with the Lord. No emotion was held back as I dug up all my disappointments, fears, questions, and bitterness against him.

For years I'd been managing those emotions, stuffing them down inside when they threatened to come to the surface. *A good Christian doesn't feel those things*, I'd say to myself time and again. *I shouldn't be feeling or thinking those thoughts.* But that day, it all came hurtling out of me. There was no way to stop it, and I didn't even try.

Every last grueling thought that had troubled and tormented me tumbled out in sobs. It was an avalanche of them, and it wasn't pretty. But there was no stopping once I got started.

When I could think of nothing more to say to him, I went silent and just lay on the bed in emptiness.

Staring at the ceiling, I let out a huge, audible sigh and waited for a long time. The relief of having said everything took a weight off, as if a boulder had been removed. I felt light for the first time in years.

Finally I said out loud, "I'm done." And I meant it.

Then, in the kindest, most loving voice imaginable, as a whisper, a breath in the wind … the Lord spoke.

"I AM," he said.

"I am with you. I am your Father. I am your Savior. I AM. I always have been.

"You've never been alone, not for one second. I've been walking right beside you, caring for you, watching over you and providing for you.

"I AM the Creator of the universe. And I AM your Creator too. I know you better than you know yourself. And I know what is best for you.

"I know you can't understand all that has happened, but even if I told you why, you wouldn't understand. You don't need to! I'm completely in control and I can handle this.

"You're making it more difficult for yourself by trying to understand me. What I want most of all is for you to trust me, to let go and let me be God, your Father.

"If you'll do that, I promise, you'll find peace, rest and blessing beyond your wildest imagination.

"But here's the catch. You can't ask me 'why' again. To do so would be sin and disobedience.

"Can you do this?"

I remember these words like it was yesterday. And I knew I was at the biggest crossroads of my life.

My flesh cried out that I had to know why. But my spirit longed to surrender and come under my Father's protection. I was tired of fighting; I was tired of trying to figure it out on my own. I desperately wanted him to rescue me from myself.

After four hours in my room that day, wrestling with God as I'd never done before, I gave in. Drawing a huge breath, I spoke out loud.

"I will not ask 'why' anymore … I promise that to you," I told him. "I don't have to know why. You don't have to explain anything to me. I give up and give you control."

Peace swept over me like a warm summer breeze as I lay on my bed after that moment of surrender. "For you died, and your life is now hidden with Christ in God." I finally knew what this verse in Colossians meant.

My life was never the same after that day. At a time when I felt utterly hopeless, God met me in a very deep, personal way.

It didn't change the circumstances of life, but he changed my heart.

Caleb's body healed from the surgery, but just a month later, he was sick with strep throat. He had barely recovered when he contracted it again. In a period of six months, he had a total of seven separate cases of it. While it was grueling to walk through, I never asked why, a huge victory for me.

Reluctant at first, our Czech pediatrician finally felt it best to remove the tonsils. But after contacting our local hospital, she found that it would be three months before there was space in the schedule to do the surgery.

We couldn't bear to see him suffer any longer, so made a plea for help. Some dear friends in the States responded, and

their doctor said he would do it for us. Shortly after the New Year in 2003, Caleb and I made a trip to Auburn, Indiana.

After being covered in prayer by the family we were staying with, we witnessed the most beautiful and unusual sunrise on our way to the hospital for surgery. Breathtaking, it reminded me of God's extravagant, and sometimes unusual, provision to care for us over the past months.

Caleb came through the surgery well, though because of his weakened body, it took longer to recover than expected. Still, we were able to fly back to Czech and be home to celebrate his tenth birthday with our family.

In the midst of Caleb's sicknesses, God brought an unexpected provision for our family that fall; a piece of land became available on which we could build a clean house for Claire's sake.

While still living at Hotel Malenovice, I noticed a piece of land nearby that had just had its price reduced. Dave called the real-estate agent and we went to see it. Standing in the tall grass on the lot, out in the farmlands with a view up to Lysá hora, the highest mountain in the range nearby, we looked at each other.

"Could this be it?" I asked. We dared to hope so, though had no idea how we would pay for it or have money to build a house on it.

We still owned our house in Havířov, but it continued to function as the office for Josiah Venture so we were not in a position to sell it. This left us with no capital for another home.

But just a few days later, during an unexpected phone call with a friend, we got our answer. After asking about the

ministry, he turned to personal issues. "How's your family?" he asked Dave.

"It's been pretty grueling this past year with all that Caleb and Claire have been through," he answered.

"What's your housing situation now? Any progress on somewhere else to live?" our friend inquired.

"We're sure we can't go back to the house in Havířov due to mold, but we can't find anything else in this area that doesn't have it too. I've just started thinking about the option of building, though I don't know how we'd do it since we still own our house and don't have resources for another one."

"You know, if you found a piece of land for sale, I'd be interested in helping you purchase it. I wouldn't have finances to help with building the house, but I'd like to help you out with the land," the friend said.

We thanked the Lord for this generous gift and for this small step forward.

Several days later another friend called. He too wanted to know about the family.

Dave told him the same story but received this response: "I wouldn't be interested in buying land for you, but if you had a piece and wanted to build, I could help you with paying for the house."

I nearly fell over when Dave recounted those phone conversations to me!

We put in an offer on the land and signed on it just a few weeks later. The process of acquiring permits and drawing up house plans with an architect lasted nine months. Finally in June 2003 a building contractor broke ground, and we were on our way to building a new house.

The gifts from our friends covered the cost of the land and half the cost of the house. Dave's dad generously loaned us the rest of the money, making it possible to build a house that was exactly what our family needed.

In April 2004 we moved in over the Easter weekend with the help of Dave's mom and dad and many friends. The house was an extraordinary extravagance from the Lord, something we'd never expected.

After nearly three years of living in a small efficiency apartment at Malenovice, experiencing all of our health difficulties, we spread out into the spaciousness and beauty of our new home, a balm for our weary souls.

God's Promise
If I look after the sparrows, I will certainly take care of you.
Luke 12:6-7

CHAPTER THIRTY-ONE **Exit 316**

"Stáž," an internship program for young Czech leaders, began in our garage in 1995. Initially developed and led by Dave, it was an intensive year of biblical and theological study, personal discipleship, ministry coaching and practical leadership training. Stáž drew young leaders from around the country who wanted to grow in their ministry skills and their personal walks with God.

Each year a group of ten to twenty young adults, both men and women, joined Stáž and committed to a year of intensive study and growth under the leadership of Dave and our team. Watching God transform these young leaders was a highlight for Dave as he and the others taught, coached, counseled, and mentored groups of leaders over the next ten years.

In May 2005, parents and friends gathered at Hotel Malenovice for the Stáž graduation of another group of students. Afterward, in the restaurant, Dave spoke with one of the dads. Striking up a conversation, Dave asked, "What do you do for a living?"

"I produce television shows for Czech Television [the government-run TV station]," Luboš Hlavsa answered.

Making polite conversation, Dave asked, "Do you want to continue in that? What are your dreams for the future?"

"Well, I'd really love to use my talents for God, and do something that would make a difference for eternity," Luboš answered.

"Wow, wouldn't it be great if there was a TV show that shared the gospel with young people here in Czech? That could reach so many who have never heard," Dave said with a touch of wistfulness.

"Are you serious?" Luboš responded.

"Well, I'm serious it's a good idea, but something like that's not possible, is it?" Dave asked.

"Maybe it is! Something like that would be worth giving all my energy to, giving my life to, even. If I pray about it, will you pray about it too?"

"Sure, I'll pray about it," Dave agreed.

But he didn't expect to hear anything back from Luboš.

However, a few months later, Luboš called Dave. "I kept thinking about our conversation, praying that God would open the door to do something like we talked about. And I may have found that door! I contacted Pavel, a friend in Czech Television, and he is willing to meet with us and talk more about our idea. Could we meet with him at Malenovice?"

A few weeks later they met in a corner of the restaurant at the hotel. Pavel had driven all the way from Prague to meet with them. He was an evangelical Christian who had headed up

Trans World radio in Czech for several years. He understood the potential for media to be used for God's work.

Amazingly, Czech Television had just hired him for a key role in their religious broadcasting department. Pavel shared that the government was concerned about the moral slide among young people and wanted to see some religious broadcasting focused on the next generation. He'd been tasked with finding a way to do that.

Most of what was being broadcast up to that point was news about the church or broadcasting of worship services, usually Catholic. There had never been a religious show designed for young people.

"We don't have much experience in this area, and you work with young people all the time," Pavel said. "If you would be willing to partner with us, we're interested in doing something new for young people."

"What kind of format?" Dave asked.

"Well, there are eight-minute, eighteen-minute and twenty-nine minute slots. I would recommend the eighteen-minute format," Pavel said. "And I would start with seventeen episodes."

This was a shock for Dave! Up until that point, he was thinking of *one* program that aired *one time*! "Are you sure you want a series?" he asked.

"Oh, yes, it's much better to fill a time slot consistently. You'll build up an audience and have greater impact," Pavel replied. "There is one problem," he added. "We are currently in a budget crisis and don't have money to pay for production. But if you'll produce the show and license it to us, we'll broadcast it for free."

Pavel continued, "Why don't you produce a pilot episode and I'll take it to Czech Television and see if they're interested in moving forward with the project."

While in theory this prospect sounded amazing, Dave had never produced anything in media before. This would be a huge leap of faith and an opportunity to trust God in ways we'd never had to before. With Luboš's expertise and Dave's vision for penetrating the culture with the gospel, they began to brainstorm about how to produce the first episode.

As they talked, they remembered that Aleš, a young man who had trusted Christ at an English camp, was currently hosting a popular MTV-type show on Czech TV. One of his best friends was Adam, a leader in a youth group our teammates had worked with for years. He was a creative writer. His dad had written for Czech Television, and the young man had starred in a movie when he was young.

As Dave and Luboš talked, they realized that out of a tiny evangelical population in Czech, there was potential for a small, gifted team to work on the pilot episode. After phone calls were made and the idea pitched, Aleš and Adam agreed to meet with Dave and Luboš for a day of concentrated work on the idea.

The concept for the show was simple. Most people are headed down the highway of life unaware that there is another option. They encounter problems along the way and deal with them on their own. What they don't know is there is an exit onto another road, the road of faith. On that road they can deal with those same problems with faith in Christ and truths of the Bible.

We called that exit "*Exit 316*" based on John 3:16. "For God so loved the world that he gave his one and only Son, that whoever believes in him shall not perish but have eternal life."

They envisioned each episode focused on a particular issue such as anger, forgiveness, depression or parents, painting a picture of the problem through interviews on the street, contemporary music and dramatization.

Then they thought, "What if we told the story of a real young person who had encountered this problem and then turned onto the way of faith, who had taken 'Exit 316'?" This person could share how that happened and what difference it made in his or her life. At the end, a mentor, someone like a pastor or youthworker, could tie up the episode with insights from God's Word.

With ideas flowing, someone proposed that two angels host the show. It sounded cliché at first, yet the more they talked they realized it would allow the angels the opportunity to consistently represent God's perspective. They could be sent to earth on a research mission, try to find out how humans were faring and conclude with God's view of the situation. Casting them as supernatural beings disguised as humans could give lots of opportunities for visual humor and interesting dialogue.

Finally, they envisioned an old VW bus carrying the angels through their travels around the Czech Republic. It sounded like this project would not only have potential to make a great spiritual impact on the youth, but it would be a lot of fun too!

After much discussion and prayer, they decided the pilot episode of *Exit 316* would be focused on forgiveness.

With Dave as the executive producer, Luboš as director, Aleš and another young woman cast as the angels, Adam writing the script, and many others giving their time and energy to the project, they set out to produce the first episode.

Two months later, they sent it in with no small amount of fear and trembling.

Was it high-enough quality? Was the message clear? Would Czech Television, a government-operated station, accept such a clear Christian message in a country with the highest percentage of atheists in the world? Could that message really reach the youth throughout the country on national television? Would it transform lives? Could it bring Christianity back into the public spotlight in this country?

We spent many hours in prayer for the project, hoping for news each day. With production on hold until news came back from Czech Television, it was an agonizing wait.

Finally, one month later news came: the series had been approved and we were cleared for seventeen episodes!

But they wanted to begin airing the show in September. How could we ever have that many episodes ready in time when it was already March?

There was an even bigger question: How could we pay for all of this?

Dave and Luboš put together a budget and found that each episode would cost $8,700 to produce. Multiplied seventeen times, it was an unbelievable sum of money that we certainly didn't have. And we didn't have much time either.

Czech Television gave them two weeks to make a decision on whether or not production would proceed. If we said yes,

it meant a commitment to produce and pay for the requested seventeen episodes.

We began to pray for a miracle.

Dave contacted various foundations and individuals about this opportunity, and asked if they would be interested in partnering with us financially. Many were enthusiastic and gave generously. But it wasn't enough to fund seventeen episodes. We sought the Lord in prayer again, asking for his leading.

One afternoon Dave was driving to visit some JV team members, and a call from an unknown number came in on his phone. Picking it up, he heard a distant voice through layers of static say, "Hi, my name is Olek*. Do you have a few minutes to talk?"

When Dave replied that he did, Olek asked him to share briefly about Josiah Venture and its history and vision.

After Dave finished his explanation, Olek asked, "Would it be possible for me to come visit you?"

"Sure," Dave said hesitantly. "But what exactly is it that you want to see?"

"I simply want to learn more," he replied through the crackling line. "I'm wondering if I can be of help to you," the man added.

"Where are you coming from?" Dave asked.

"My wife and I live in Ukraine. I'm Ukrainian by descent, American by passport."

Dave replied, "Well, you won't have too far to travel then. When would you like to come?"

"A week from now," Olek replied. "Let's meet in Prague," he continued. "And bring your wife. I want to meet her too. I'll

* Names changed for privacy

send you our arrival information. Could you book a hotel for us? Then I'd like to travel across the country with you and see your training center. We'll stay for three days. See you soon."

When Dave got home, he told me about the mystery phone call.

"What exactly does he want?" I asked with curiosity.

"Honestly, I have no idea. He gave no clue about who he is and why he wants to meet with us. But it's so out of the blue that it makes me wonder what's going on, and if God is somehow orchestrating this. I think we should go and find out who he is and why he wants to meet us."

Always up for an adventure, a week later Dave and I drove to Prague to meet Olek and his wife.

It felt a bit like something out of a spy movie as we met them on a cobblestoned street in the city and headed toward a restaurant tucked into the walls of Prague's castle. Throughout the meal, Dave and I tried to find out more about Olek and what he was doing there.

But our questions were deflected as he peppered us with his own. He seemed to want to know everything: how we met, how the ministry started, our visions and goals, what our kids were like. It was one of the most unusual conversations we'd ever had.

Climbing into our car with them the next morning brought another barrage of questions as we traveled four hours toward home. During the drive, information about who he was and why he'd come to see us trickled out.

Olek represented a family foundation that has no front door, meaning there is no way to approach them, contact them, meet with them or submit grant proposals for potential funding.

Instead, they have representatives working in regions around the world asking questions about leaders and ministries, contacting ones they think have potential interest to the family.

Since this foundation works completely anonymously, we knew nothing about them and had no previous contact. We didn't know how they heard about us, or what it was that made them interested in pursuing more information. Even as we found out who Olek was and why he was there, we didn't know what the family foundation was interested in or what their financial capacity was.

All we knew was that he and his wife had been sent to visit us. So we shared our lives, dreams and visions for reaching young people with the gospel throughout Central and Eastern Europe.

Near the end of their time with us, Dave shared about the opportunity with *Exit 316*, and what had transpired over the past months with the opportunity to air a Christian show on national television for young people.

Olek lit up.

"Our foundation is particularly interested in innovative ways to get the gospel out through media," he said with interest. "How much would you need to fund this project?"

Doing some quick math in his head, Dave answered, "It will take $148,000 for the production of seventeen episodes. But already Czech Television has talked to us about another twenty-six episodes, so our need is potentially even more than that.

"With such an unprecedented opportunity to penetrate the country with biblical truth through *Exit 316*, I think God is asking me to trust him for $375,000 for the production of forty-three episodes," Dave shared. Sensing the leading of the

Spirit, he added, "But there is another aspect of it that we'd like to do as well."

Just a few weeks earlier Dave had been in Costa Rica for a Global Youth Initiative conference. There he had a conversation with Dann Spader about the potential of *Exit 316*.

"What's most important is not what people see on television but the conversation they have with their friends afterward. How can you equip the church to use this opportunity to share Christ with their friends?" Dann had asked Dave.

The wheels in Dave's head began to turn as he contemplated this thought. The show would reach people with the truths of the gospel. But local churches across the country could also use it in a parallel evangelism campaign. Dreaming about how to make that a reality, he even had a name for it: *Turbo 316*.

"We see the parallel campaign as absolutely essential for the long-term fruit of the project," Dave shared with Olek.

"We'd like to develop a leadership team to train local churches to use materials designed for discussion after each episode. We'd also like to print special edition *Exit 316* Bibles for those who participate in the small groups."

Dave continued, "A project of this nature has never been done in this region, and, if done well, could open the door for other similar initiatives. We don't know how long this window of opportunity will stay open, and we think it's crucial to use the open doors while they are available."

Dave finished by saying, "I am convinced that this show could put spiritual awareness back into the marketplace and make lasting change for the sake of God's kingdom in this

country." He then added, "And to answer your question: I think it will take $640,000 to make it happen."

Dave sat back, wondering if he'd cast too big of a vision for this unknown foundation. We waited for Olek's response.

He was silent. We felt the enormity of that amount, and the impossibility of the situation. But we were also confident in God's ability to work a miracle.

Finally Olek asked, "How soon do you need to know before you can move ahead?"

"Czech Television needs to know within two weeks," Dave replied.

"Normally our foundation doesn't work that fast. But I'll see what I can do."

With no other leads for such a huge amount of finances, we prayed and waited, unsure of what Olek and the family foundation's response would be.

Two weeks later, in another crackling phone call from Ukraine, Olek said to Dave, "The family has approved a one-for-one matching grant of $323,000 and $26,000 toward phase one of *Turbo 316*. We pray God will continue to bless you and your colleagues in this new venture to reach the young people of Czech Republic with the good news of the risen Lord."

With that news, we knew we had the green light to move ahead.

Exit 316 would be a reality.

God's Promise
I hear you when you ask for anything according to my will.
1 John 5:14

CHAPTER THIRTY-TWO *Miracle on TV*

Dave, Luboš and the rest of the team immediately sailed into production mode. The first six episodes had to be turned in to Czech Television by the end of July. With just three months to work, everyone went into overtime mode.

Scripts were written and rewritten, additional casting took place, mentors were found, filming occurred across the country, edits were made and the stories of young people were discovered.

It was an all-out effort to get those first six episodes completed by the end of July. The team worked long and hard throughout the summer, completing them and moving on to the next episodes.

At the same time, Dave was writing small group material to be used for *Turbo 316*. Soon a new team was in place to begin training churches on how to use the materials, and they began

traveling the country. People were excited about the potential to reach their friends and family through this unique opportunity.

One leader from a church in Opava called Petr, the leader of the Turbo team. "We just heard about the *Turbo 316* project and want to start five evangelistic small groups. Can we get the materials for our Exit clubs?"

Petr asked him, "When do you need them?"

The man replied, "Tomorrow!"

"I can't get them to you that fast in the mail," Petr said.

"Can I drive down and pick them up?" the man replied.

Petr said yes. The man immediately got in his car and drove two and a half hours one way to pick up the materials, so that he'd have them for the next night after the premiere aired.

A woman took a stack of *Exit 316* flyers to the grocery store where she worked and talked with every person who came through her line that day. She later told us that she'd never been able to talk to people so openly about the Lord, but the fact that this was going to be on national television made it very easy.

She said that many of the people she talked to had teenagers, and almost all of them were having problems with them. When they heard the show was focused on issues young people face, they said they would make sure they watched it with their kids.

On September 6, 2006, the first episode premiered on national television across the country.

We watched it at Hotel Malenovice, on a big screen in the meeting room. Before it aired, I drove into town to pick up pizza. When I saw people walking in town, I began to pray that many would head home and turn on their televisions.

As I sat waiting for the pizzas, I prayed for all those across the country who might be returning home from work or school at that moment and turning on their televisions to see what was airing. I prayed they would find *Exit 316*, and that God would begin to stir something supernatural across the country as they watched.

When I got back to the hotel and walked into the meeting room where everyone was gathered, I felt a chill go through me. I wasn't prepared for how emotional I would feel as I sat watching the clock tick down until it was 6:05 p.m. I had tears in my eyes for most of the eighteen minutes of the show. This was more than just a "premiere"—this was a historic moment in the Czech Republic.

Of course, I'd already seen the episode several times. It wasn't the content that brought the tears; it was the tremendous significance of that watershed moment. I felt that one day we would be able to look back and say, "The spiritual climate of the country was different from that time on."

Twenty of us gathered for the premiere and afterward had a time of prayer for *Exit 316*. We prayed for all the small groups that were happening across the country at that moment, for those who had just viewed it, for the team who would continue in production of more episodes, and for a spiritual awakening in this country.

They were bold prayers of faith, but I felt certain God would answer them.

When Dave started to pray, he was overcome with emotion. I sat beside him, holding his hand, feeling his tears splash on us. It was a sacred moment. Though filled with emotion, he pressed

through his prayer, asking God to do more than we could ask or imagine. Others joined him and then it was quiet.

It felt right to me that we let it be the holy moment that it was. The airing of such a straightforward Christian program on national television was so incomprehensible, especially in the most atheistic country in the world. The presence of the Lord was there throughout the premiere, but I especially felt it in the quiet of that moment.

And then it was over and people moved on into regular life again. I cleaned up the pizza and drinks, talked to a few people and headed home. The evening was finished.

But the work of *Exit 316* had only begun!

In the following months, forty-three episodes were produced and aired. Czech Television aired them not just once a week, but three times, and made them available for online streaming.

On average, 150,000 to 200,000 viewings were counted for each episode. With only an estimated 10,000 believers in the country, we knew that many non-believers were watching the show.

During that year, more than five hundred *Exit 316* small groups were led. We heard story after story of young people and adults putting their faith in Christ as they studied the Bible with their friends.

Online discussions took place on the *Exit 316* Web site, as people were curious and wanted to know more. Our vision and dream of bringing the topic of spiritual things into the public marketplace was beginning to happen.

But such a significant thrust for the gospel never goes forward without opposition. *Exit 316* was under attack as well.

Within four weeks of the premiere, Czech Television let us know the show was under threat of cancellation. Meetings occurred, discussions were had, opinions were given and many prayed.

Amazingly, despite a segment of the population being against such a blatantly Christian show, Czech Television made the brave decision to continue airing *Exit 316*.

In December of that year, the Exit team was invited to the Ecumenical Council of Churches award event in Prague. To their surprise, they were presented with the only award of the night: the "Best Ecumenical Act of 2006" for the production and airing of *Exit 316*.

It was thrilling to watch God do something so far beyond what we could have ever imagined, as he moved in the lives of people across the country, in believers and non-believers alike. *Exit 316* spurred the believers on to be bold with their faith and personal testimony, and non-believers had the opportunity to hear the message of Christ in a way that was relevant to their lives.

The team worked hard that year, producing the shows and equipping churches to use them. It was an intense year, but as the last episode aired, we rejoiced in the miracle that had occurred in the Czech Republic.

Yet we had only begun to see how God intended to use *Exit 316* to impact the lives of young people across the nation and the region.

God's Promise
The good things that I have planned for you are too many
to count.
Psalm 40:5

CHAPTER THIRTY-THREE

Gospel in Schools

A total of forty-one episodes of *Exit 316* aired over nine months in 2006–2007. All the finances needed for production had been generously given, and the *Turbo* project had resulted in many new believers, as well as ongoing small groups that used the show to share Christ.

The final two episodes were due to air in the fall because of programming issues with Czech Television, which was fine with us. It would be another opportunity for truth and biblical principles to be aired again, along with reruns they planned.

Everyone was exhausted from the intense year and a half that it had taken to see this project through. Many hours of labor, by literally hundreds of people, had gone into making and using *Exit 316* to penetrate the country with biblical messages about faith and the difference it could make in someone's life.

We celebrated with the core team at our house in July that year, praising God for the evidence of his work to see this project through.

And then news came from Czech Television.

"Would you consider doing another year of episodes?" they asked.

Not only had it been a success for us in spiritual terms, it was also a success for them. Those in leadership sensed that changes were occurring in the fabric of society and wanted to see that continue.

Our team knew it would take time to gear up for another round of production, but everyone was interested in continuing.

"If we took this coming year to prepare, do you think they'd keep their offer open?" one of the team members asked.

Dave and Luboš approached Czech Television with their proposition to produce forty new episodes. They proposed that we would again pay for the cost of production, and thus retain rights to the show, while they would pay for the broadcast. They agreed and set the date to air the new season of *Exit 316* in September 2008.

Once again, finances had to be raised, scripts written, new casting completed. Production began later that summer, even though it would be a year before episodes would air. The team was thankful to have a little more breathing room than the year before, when episodes were being finished just weeks before they aired.

The same foundation that had anonymously given to the first season again gave generously. Other foundations and donors contributed as well to cover the costs of production and a new round of *Turbo 316*.

Wanting to build on what had happened the previous season, Dave had a new dream for *Exit 316*'s second season.

In June, the youth leader at our church in Frýdlant held an annual outreach event for young people in our town. An innovative and creative leader, Bogdan Lach put up a tent on an empty lot and ran a program all day long to reach out to students. Prior to the event, he had envisioned a live evening concert to draw in youth, and asked our son Tyler if he would be interested in being the artist for the evening. Though Tyler had never done anything like that before, he enlisted the help of his brother Caleb, and the two of them put together a list of fifty songs that they began to prepare.

Bogdan wanted the concert to have a "coffeehouse" feel, with music playing for two to three hours nonstop. Tyler and Caleb spent hours in preparation, but were excited about the prospect of headlining a concert venue.

One of the things that I loved about raising our kids in Czech, and as missionary kids, is that they often had opportunities like this: to do unusual things that stretched them as people and built faith into their lives. Knowing they didn't have the resources within themselves, they had to trust God for these types of things and believe that he'd come through for them.

The outreach drew hundreds of people during the day, and that evening we listened for over two hours as our two sons played music while people talked and enjoyed the warm, open atmosphere.

As I stood in the tent feeling proud of our sons, Dave stood with wheels turning in his head.

"What if we could do something like this across the country, and use it evangelistically?" he asked me as the boys played up front. "In conjunction with another year of *Exit 316* broadcasts, I wonder what it would be like to get into schools with a band that could give concerts, but also speak on the topics that were being covered in the episodes? It could be like a promotional tour for *Exit 316*."

As production ramped up again for new *Exit 316* episodes, Dave continued to think about this idea.

"Where would we get a band? How would we pay for it? What would we call it?" Dave asked me time and again.

But the biggest question of all was: "Could we get into the schools?"

In February 2008 Dave was in the States for a Josiah Venture board meeting. After reports and updates on various aspects of the ministry, the board gave Dave time to share his heart, vision and thoughts on the future.

"What have you been thinking about recently?" Philip, our board chair, asked him.

Dave began to share about his dream for a promotional tour for *Exit 316*. "I've already had the team checking to see if we could get into schools, and we can! There is an open door that would allow us to be in high schools for an entire day," he explained.

"The Czech government has tasked high schools with providing an annual assembly, a full day set aside for a prevention program. They want the students to get information about things like abstinence, drugs, sex, and moral issues. High schools are now required to annually provide this for their students, but the

administrators and teachers don't know what to do. Imagine what we could offer them!"

"What are you proposing?" one of the board members asked.

"Well, here's my idea. What if we get a rock band, some great guys who are sold out for Jesus, and we bring them over to Czech for say, eight weeks. They'd be the Exit 316 band and could tour the country doing assemblies and promoting the show.

"If we teamed them up with speakers, some of the leaders we've been training who could talk to the students on various topics, we'd let the band build relationships and give concerts, providing a whole package for the schools to fulfill their requirements. It seems like this would be a win-win situation for us and for the schools," Dave said.

"There's just one thing I can't figure out," he added.

"What's that?" asked another board member.

"I have no idea where to find this rock band!" said Dave with a chuckle.

The board was enthusiastic about Dave's vision, and told him to press ahead and see if there was any way to make it a reality.

After the meeting was over, Scott, one of the board members, approached Dave. "You're not going to believe this, but I think I actually might know a band who could do this," he said.

"You're kidding!" Dave exclaimed. "Who do you have in mind?"

Scott then shared about a young man from his church who had been touring for ten years with a band that he and his brother had started called Dizmas.

"Let me talk to him and see if there's any interest. I think they just got a contract with a recording label in Nashville, but I'm not so sure that's what the Lord has in store for Zach Zegan. He's a unique guy, and I think the Lord wants to do something more with him than make his band famous. I'll get together with him as soon as I can and get back to you."

Three weeks later, Zach was sitting in our living room in the Czech Republic to have a conversation about what this could look like. And six short months later, God orchestrated something we could never have imagined.

In October, Zach brought his rock band, Dizmas, from California, and they began what we called "Exit Tour." Along with a group of Czech lecturers, Dizmas went into public high schools through the door opened by the government, and were able to spend an entire day with high school students in their environment.

At each high school, Dizmas gave a short concert to begin the day, and then a group of Czech lecturers, as well as members of the band, gave seminars on relevant topics, including discussions on the new episodes of *Exit 316*, which had just started airing for the second season.

The response was overwhelmingly positive. Students were highly receptive to what they heard, and attended after-school activities offered by local churches, anxious to talk personally with the band after they openly shared their testimonies of faith in God and how he had changed their lives.

Over the next two years, Zach and the band came four times from California to travel throughout Czech with the Exit Tour team. Each time they experienced unprecedented openness and

receptiveness from teenagers, as well as school administrations, to the message of how life is different when you have faith in God.

After a total of eighty-three *Exit 316* episodes, with over eight million viewings during its two-year run, the show wrapped up production. It had surpassed our expectations, and begun a change in the spiritual climate of the country.

But this was not the end of its impact. Exit Tour continued, and over the past eight years a band and team has traveled the Czech Republic sharing in public schools the life-changing message of what happens when you take the way of faith in Jesus Christ.

Exit Tour also spread into neighboring countries Slovakia and Poland, even though the show was not aired in their languages. But the results were the same: students were interested in hearing more about what faith in God really means.

Because the gospel couldn't be shared during class time, students were always invited to after-school events where the band and lecturers were free to share their faith.

One of our JV staff in Slovakia could sense a hunger in the students he was lecturing during an Exit Tour. After speaking about family and relationships, and how those can be different when God is involved, he invited students to stay during the break and hear the gospel and what it means to have a personal relationship with God.

On the first break, just fifteen minutes long, he shared the plan of salvation and gave students an opportunity to respond. Fourteen students raised their hands, saying they wanted to begin a relationship with Jesus. He took a picture with them before the break ended, overwhelmed by what had just happened.

After another lecture, he gave the same invitation: "Stay during the break and I'll tell you how you can have a personal relationship with God."

Many in the group stayed, and this time thirteen put their faith in Christ. He captured another photo with that group, mostly boys, who were hungry for something more in their lives. During that Exit Tour, an unbelievable total of eighty-three students indicated that they put their faith in Christ.

Exit Tour continues to be one of our most fruitful efforts in bringing the gospel to young people.

God's Promise
My children will overcome the world through their faith.
1 John 5:4

CHAPTER THIRTY-FOUR *Saying Yes*

As often happens when a new thrust of the gospel is launched, our family experienced many different types of attack over the years. Sleepless nights, odd sicknesses, threats from non-believing parents, stolen items, broken appliances, car problems and hospitalizations often co-incided with times when the ministry was moving forward into new territory.

As Exit Tour began, our son Caleb, fifteen at the time, began to suffer excruciating pain again in his stomach.

After many unsuccessful attempts to discover what was causing the pain, he and I left for the States to seek additional medical help. We spent four weeks at a children's hospital, un-dergoing tests, only to be told in the end that he was suffering from chronic pain that would most likely be a part of his life forever.

Still looking for answers, we switched to a gluten-free, no carbohydrate diet that brought some relief. But varying degrees of pain continued over the next four years.

The summer after graduation from Czech high school, he worked at Gull Lake Ministries, a Christian family camp in Michigan. Without explanation, the pain increased to such intensity that he was unable to continue working. After much prayer, Dave flew to the States and accompanied him to Cleveland Clinic in Ohio for more testing.

God had led them to a doctor who pioneered a very specific test for identifying sources of pain in the stomach. On the last of four grueling days of tests, he administered a final one.

The results from this test shed light on the mystery of Caleb's suffering.

After giving him an epidural, they performed different blocks on various sets of nerves, noting what caused his pain to increase or decrease. When they got to the muscular wall of his abdomen, Dr. Cheng discovered a particular set of nerves that had been damaged during Caleb's intestinal surgery ten years earlier in Czech.

He came out to the waiting room to see Dave immediately following the test to say, "I'm glad to tell you that we've finally found the cause of Caleb's problem. And I have a solution to help him."

After a prolonged, expensive and often frustrating search over many years, it was an immense relief to finally know what was wrong and to be given hope for healing.

Dr. Cheng went on to explain a procedure for injecting medication into the spine as often as needed, which would essentially put the nerves to sleep and allow them time to heal. While he said it could possibly take three to five years before seeing long-lasting results, he said the body is amazing and that he's seen even worse nerve damage heal with time.

Today, four years later, Caleb hasn't needed an injection for eleven months. That's a record. In the beginning, the medication lasted just ten to twelve weeks at a time, so we're encouraged by this progress. Our hope and prayer continues to be that over time those nerves will fully heal, and that he will not live with pain indefinitely.

But what if he does?

This is something I have wrestled with for many years. Why does God allow suffering? Are God's promises true, even when life is difficult? How do I trust God when I don't see anything happening? Do my prayers make a difference? What should my response be to trials?

Many more qualified than I have written papers, articles and books on this weighty topic. But it is simply the Bible, God's message to us, that has brought the most understanding and comfort to me over the years as I've watched various members of my family, including myself, suffer from physical pain.

> Dear friends, do not be surprised at the painful trial you are suffering, as though something strange were happening to you. But rejoice that you participate in the sufferings of Christ, so that you may be overjoyed when his glory is revealed.
> 1 Peter 4:12-13

> Be self-controlled and alert. Your enemy the devil prowls around like a roaring lion looking for someone to devour. Resist him, standing firm in the faith,

because you know that your brothers throughout the world are undergoing the same kind of sufferings.
1 Peter 5:8-9

And the God of all grace, who called you to his eternal glory in Christ, after you have suffered a little while, will himself restore you and make you strong, firm and steadfast. To him be the power for ever and ever. Amen.
1 Peter 5:10-11

We have endured open-heart surgery on Dave, and Claire's eye problems and desperate fight for life when she was young. I've suffered for many years with severe migraines that landed me in bed scores of times and sent me to the hospital as well. And then, of course, there has been Caleb's thirteen-year pain journey, along with many other difficulties for all of us.

I cling to the hope that God is not surprised by our sufferings, and even uses it for our good.

Just three days ago, I suffered yet another brutal migraine that put me in bed for days, unable to write, unable to do even the simplest of tasks.

But rather than fight against my body or be angry, instead I embraced it, saying yes to God's ways as I've learned to do these past years, thanking him for his presence in the midst of pain. Of course, I take my medication to ease the pain (which works sometimes, but not always), and I consult with my doctor to make sure there is no deeper cause for the migraine (so far there hasn't been).

But I also relax into the arms of my Father who knows what I am suffering. And I pray.

I am no longer surprised by the painful trials I suffer. Instead I cling to the Lord, trusting that he knows what he's doing. Many years ago, after my crisis of faith when Caleb was ill, I stopped asking why or questioning God. I literally just said "No" to that endless cycle of asking "Why?"

Rather, I set my heart on asking what he wants me to pray for, what he wants me to think about, what his plan is for me while I wait for his way to be known.

I've learned that anxiety gets me nowhere, that worry is not only harmful to me but a sin, and that if I'll entrust myself into my loving Father's care, I'll be a lot better off, even if I'm suffering from pain or watching others suffer.

I also know that I'm part of something bigger going on in the spiritual realm.

Sometimes I think the Lord wants me to take my place and play a part in his bigger plan: the redemption of his people around the world. I get to pray and stand guard alongside him for all that he's doing to call and bring people to himself. That's a privilege, and I take it very seriously when I find myself in that position, able to do nothing more than pray. As if that's a small thing!

When I've knelt by my kids' beds through the years as they suffered, when I sat by Dave's side in a Czech hospital after heart surgery, when I've been under the covers of my own bed in excruciating pain, my "yes" to God has brought an unspeakable joy of calling out to him on behalf of many. It's been a privilege to pray for an outpouring of grace and mercy for family, friends and people around the world.

As I've grown in my trust, understanding and knowledge of God and his promises, I've sought to keep saying yes no matter the cost. There are many days when I have chosen to believe his promises in the midst of seeing no sign of them being true.

But the joy of following him and feeling his pleasure when I've responded with my yes has far outweighed the difficulties. The only changes I would make in my life would be to have said yes sooner and more often.

What about you? Are there areas of your life where you need to say yes to God? What's keeping you from it? What will it mean if you do? What will it mean if you don't?

Will you have to give up something? Is he asking you to go somewhere you don't want to go? Do you need to lay down something you've been clinging to? Is there something he wants you to stand up for?

Is he asking you to tell the truth when a lie seems easier? Will saying yes be costly? Does it seem too painful to say yes? Will the future be unknown if you do? Will you lose something if you don't?

And finally: Why wouldn't you say yes?

I've often asked myself that question and wrestled with my own yes to God. Saying yes can be uncomfortable, even painful. It can be costly and time consuming. It can mean giving up something that I wanted, or doing something that I don't want to do.

But here is the secret I've learned over forty years of my journey of faith:

> *My yes begins with God's YES.*
> *Yes, I chose you before the foundations of the world.*
> *Yes, I love you with an everlasting love.*

Yes, I sent my Son to die for you and give you life.

Yes, I destroyed the barrier between us and gave you access to me through Jesus.

Yes, I have blessed you with every spiritual blessing in Christ.

Yes, I will supply all your needs in Christ Jesus.

These, and so many more, are his promises to us.

These are the ones that assure us of his constant love, care, nurture, strength, and protection. We have nothing to fear by saying yes to him. He is completely for us as we lay down our lives for him.

Yet, many settle for less than yes. They don't say yes, because it's scary and risky. There is a sense of loss, a surrendering and giving up of control.

But God is faithful. Believe that truth. As we say our amen and yes, his promises become yes, and we can rest in them.

All those questions you're asking him? If it relates to a promise in Christ Jesus, then it is a yes from him.

Yes, you are loved.

Yes, you are forgiven.

Yes, he will use you.

Yes, he has a plan for your life.

Yes, he will never leave you.

Yes, you have a home in heaven.

All those are answered yes in Christ Jesus.

And this gives us the courage and the foundation to speak our "amen," to give our wholehearted "yes" to all of God's ways, plans, thoughts and requests.

Remember this: your yes is always preceded by *HIS* yes. He said it first.

Can I say to him anything less than yes?

God's Promise
For no matter how many promises God has made, they are "Yes"
in Christ. And so through him we speak the "Amen"
to the glory of God.
2 Corinthians 1:20

He Is Faithful

When Josiah Venture began in 1993, there were three couples working in two countries. Today, in 2016, there are 320 missionaries serving in thirteen countries of Central and Eastern Europe.

The people on this dedicated, gifted, servant-hearted, multinational team are powerfully sharing their lives and the gospel in so many creative and amazing ways: through English camps, sports, music, media, Exit Tours, leadership training, church planting, teaching in schools, discipleship, retreats, books, seminars, conferences and personal relationships.

We are so thankful for this dedicated group of servants who pour out their lives for the sake of the gospel as it goes out to young people across our region.

With gratefulness to God, thousands upon thousands of young people have put their faith in Christ over the past years across Central and Eastern Europe, and that thrills us! We

rejoice in the movement of God that is spreading throughout this region, impacting the lives of many with the good news of Jesus Christ. We continue to pray for hundreds of thousands, even millions and more, to know, follow and serve him.

Our children, Tyler, Caleb, and Claire, are all in the States now. After completing thirteen years of schooling in the Czech school system, they went on to higher education in the United States.

Tyler finished his degree at Moody Bible Institute in 2013 and now attends Trinity Evangelical Divinity School in Deerfield, Illinois, studying for his master's degree in Old Testament and Semitic Languages. He and his wife, Lara, plan to return to the Czech Republic to serve as missionaries with Josiah Venture in 2017. Our darling grandson, Judah, was born to them in November 2015.

Caleb graduated from Moody Bible Institute as well. With a heart for the world and a desire to change it for the sake of Christ, he also plans to be back in Europe as a missionary serving with Josiah Venture. He met Haley, the girl of his dreams, when he was fifteen, and they are now married and living in Colorado, dreaming, planning, and praying about their future.

Claire finished high school in Czech in 2013 and left for Chicago also to study at Moody Bible Institute. With a heart for kids, she is studying children's ministry and desires to share and show Christ wherever God leads, although she hopes it is back to serve in Europe someday. She will graduate in December 2016.

Dave continues as the president and visionary for Josiah Venture. After twenty-three years in the Czech Republic and

thirty-five years of ministry, he is still passionate and compelled to see the gospel go out to young people, that they would come to faith in Christ, be discipled and then trained as leaders for the next generation.

And me? After more than thirty years on the mission field, I am content with my calling to follow Jesus, be available for whatever he asks of me, to stand in prayer for his movement among young people across Central and Eastern Europe, to say an unreserved yes whenever he calls and to believe his promises every day of my life.

God's Promise
Hold fast to the hope you confess, for I am faithful to keep
my promises.
Hebrews 10:23

Acknowledgments

With all my heart, I give my deepest thanks and praise to the Lord, the One who gave his life so that I might live: I love you, Lord, with all my heart, soul, mind, and strength. Thank you for choosing me to be your daughter, for the truth of your promises, and for calling me into the greatest life I could ever imagine. Thank you for saying yes to me, so I could say yes to you.

Aside from the Lord, the greatest gift in my life is Dave, my husband of nearly thirty years: I love you for never taking your eyes off Jesus, your deep and unswerving faith, your intentional and sacrificial love, and for leading our family to trust God. Sharing life with you is better than I ever dreamed of. This book would never have been written without you.

To my precious children, Tyler, Lara, Caleb, Haley, and Claire: Three of you I birthed, two of you are grafted in by marriage – and I simply love all of you more than words could ever say! Thank you for walking with God, for making great decisions in life, for choosing to lay your lives down for the sake

of the gospel, for being so much fun to hang out with, and for wanting to come back and serve with us in JV. You bring me so much joy and delight!

For our dear first grandson, Judah: Oh, how you have my heart! I pray you'll love and follow Jesus like your daddy and mommy, Papa and Nonnie, aunts and uncles, and great-grand-parents. You are so loved.

The Josiah Venture family that continues to give their lives for the sake of the gospel to young people across Central and Eastern Europe: Thank you for your bold faith, for engaging in dynamic community, for doing everything with God-honoring excellence, for your deep integrity, and your commitment to indigenous empowerment. You are an amazing family and it's a privilege to do life with you!

There are so many of you who have served, and are serving, with us whose names I couldn't mention in the book. One of my editor's comments was, "Missionaries sure know a lot of people." That was a nice way of saying, "You can't say the name of every person who has ever served in JV." I wanted to. But you know who are, and I hope you know how truly thankful I am for each and every one of you.

Both sets of our parents, Jim and Linda France, Dick and Margaret Patty, have truly been sacrificial in loving us as we served God a continent away from them. Thank you for your endless prayers, timely visits, generous gifts, and deep care expressed to us many times over. We are who we are today because of you.

Family, friends and supporters: We are deeply indebted to you for your generosity and care for our family all these years.

Thank you for believing God with us for his movement across Central and Eastern Europe.

To Laurelwood Baptist Church, Vancouver, Washington; Faith Evangelical Free Church, Fort Collins, Colorado; Bethany Evangelical Free Church, Littleton, Colorado; Grace Church of DuPage, Warrenville, Illinois; Christ Community Church, St. Charles, Illinois: a special thank you for graciously and generously standing with us as partners in the gospel for more than thirty years.

Our prayer warriors who have spent countless hours in prayer for us: Thank you with all my heart for going to the Lord on our behalf, praying us through many difficulties, believing God for his redemptive work here, and standing in faith for his movement in this region of the world. Your crowns in heaven will have many jewels for your service behind the scenes.

Bob and Sherry: Sea Grace in North Hampton was *the* perfect place to begin writing this book. So thankful for your kindness and generosity to let us stay in your lovely home and use the swim spa!

Steve and Polly, Foster and Lynn: Teton Pines was the perfect place to *finish* writing this book! Thank you for letting us live for a month in your beautiful home in snowy Jackson, Wyoming. It blessed us!

Chris Hudson, Robin Merrill and the superb editors at Peachtree Editorial: your expertise, editing, excellence and overall kindness in this book-writing process meant the world to me. Thank you for being endlessly patient and persistent in seeing it through to the end.

Barry Adams: Thank you for your kindness in allowing me to quote the promises of God from your website, 365Promises.com. They continue to be an encouragement to me.

And last, a thank you to these friends who have walked through life with me and made a lasting mark through their kindness, prayers, input, love, generosity and care: My brother, Mike, Michelle, Jim & Jan, Jim & Barbara, Dan & Laura, David & Joyce, Jay & Jerri, Brian & Lori, Ruth, Bill & Jeannette, Susan, Pam, Muriel, Jo, Warren & Shirley, Gordon & Sherrie, Greg & Terri, Josh & Kristi, Tammy, Karen F., Theresa, Dick & Judi, Bob & Judy, Scott & Karla, Frank & Wendy, Scott & Emily, Bob & Manette, Steve & Cari, Debbie, Janet, Ellie, Daryl & Jean, Tom & Carol, Ken & Andrea, Jim & Lina, Greg & Heidi, Mel & Amy, Becca, Bret & Sarah, Ingrid, Dušan & Danča, Barča, Paul & Sharon, Petr & Lauren, Jonny & Lisa, Brian & Aleisha, Katka, Pavel & Jana, Martina, Mike & Linda, Linda B., Jerry & Kris, Peter & Mary, Steve & Polly, Ginny, Laurie, Kris & John, Rennie, Kelly, Charlie & Suzi, and our cousin, Jenny, who says she'll be the first to buy my book!

My dearest family and friends, thank you for inspiring, encouraging and challenging me to say "no less than yes" to the Lord. I love you all so much!

~Connie

Made in the
USA
Columbia, SC